DISEASES & DISORDERS

Exercise Addiction

Leanne K. Currie-McGhee

LUCENT BOOKS
A part of Gale, Cengage Learning

Detroit • New York • San Francisco • New Haven, Conn • Waterville, Maine • London

LIBRARY OF CONGRESS CATALOGING-IN-PUBLICATION DATA

Currie-McGhee, L. K. (Leanne K.)
  Exercise addiction / by Leanne Currie-McGhee.
    p. cm. -- (Diseases & disorders)
  Includes bibliographical references and index.
  ISBN 978-1-4205-0551-1 (hardcover : alk. paper)
  1. Exercise addiction--Juvenile literature. I. Title.
  RC569.5.E94C87 2011
  616.85'84--dc22

               2010039535

Lucent Books
27500 Drake Rd.
Farmington Hills, MI 48331

ISBN-13: 978-1-4205-0551-1
ISBN-10: 1-4205-0551-3

Printed in the United States of America
1 2 3 4 5 6 7 15 14 13 12 11

Printed by Bang Printing, Brainerd, MN, 1ˢᵗ Ptg., 01/2011

Table of Contents

"The Most Difficult Puzzles Ever Devised"

Charles Best, one of the pioneers in the search for a cure for diabetes, once explained what it is about medical research that intrigued him so. "It's not just the gratification of knowing one is helping people," he confided, "although that probably is a more heroic and selfless motivation. Those feelings may enter in, but truly, what I find best is the feeling of going toe to toe with nature, of trying to solve the most difficult puzzles ever devised. The answers are there somewhere, those keys that will solve the puzzle and make the patient well. But how will those keys be found?"

Since the dawn of civilization, nothing has so puzzled people—and often frightened them, as well—as the onset of illness in a body or mind that had seemed healthy before. A seizure, the inability of a heart to pump, the sudden deterioration of muscle tone in a small child—being unable to reverse such conditions or even to understand why they occur was unspeakably frustrating to healers. Even before there were names for such conditions, even before they were understood at all, each was a reminder of how complex the human body was, and how vulnerable.

While our grappling with understanding diseases has been frustrating at times, it has also provided some of humankind's most heroic accomplishments. Alexander Fleming's accidental discovery in 1928 of a mold that could be turned into penicillin has resulted in the saving of untold millions of lives. The isolation of the enzyme insulin has reversed what was once a death sentence for anyone with diabetes. There have been great strides in combating conditions for which there is not yet a cure, too. Medicines can help AIDS patients live longer, diagnostic tools such as mammography and ultrasounds can help doctors find tumors while they are treatable, and laser surgery techniques have made the most intricate, minute operations routine.

This "toe-to-toe" competition with diseases and disorders is even more remarkable when seen in a historical continuum. An astonishing amount of progress has been made in a very short time. Just two hundred years ago, the existence of germs as a cause of some diseases was unknown. In fact, it was less than 150 years ago that a British surgeon named Joseph Lister had difficulty persuading his fellow doctors that washing their hands before delivering a baby might increase the chances of a healthy delivery (especially if they had just attended to a diseased patient)!

Each book in Lucent's Diseases and Disorders series explores a disease or disorder and the knowledge that has been accumulated (or discarded) by doctors through the years. Each book also examines the tools used for pinpointing a diagnosis, as well as the various means that are used to treat or cure a disease. Finally, new ideas are presented—techniques or medicines that may be on the horizon.

Frustration and disappointment are still part of medicine, for not every disease or condition can be cured or prevented. But the limitations of knowledge are being pushed outward constantly; the "most difficult puzzles ever devised" are finding challengers every day.

Out of Control

Can a person ever exercise too much? At first thought, the answer seems like no. Doctors and other health care professionals recommend that people exercise every day to keep healthy and are more concerned that people are not exercising enough. "The benefits of regular aerobic (endurance) exercise for the general population, and especially people with heart disease, are well known," writes Paul Egan, exercise physiologist at the Cleveland Clinic Foundation. "There have been countless medical research studies that show exercise may improve: endurance and cardiovascular fitness, mood and 'feelings of well being,' cholesterol levels, risk of developing diabetes, blood sugar control for diabetics, weight control, blood pressure control, stress management, and even risks for certain types of cancer."[1]

Despite all of the benefits of exercise, there is a point where a person can exercise too much. This happens when exercise becomes the center of a person's life and he or she is endangering his or her emotional and physical state. People who put exercise before anything else are considered exercise addicts or compulsive exercisers.

Addicts exercise even if they are injured or sick and will choose exercise over other social or work obligations no matter how important these other obligations are. "Exercise abuse [also called exercise addiction or excessive exercise] is a compulsion to exercise, where you feel you can't stop," says Kenneth Littlefield, a psychologist at the Arizona-based Remuda Ranch, a treatment facility for people who have eating disorders. "The part where it becomes an addiction is where you need increasing amounts to feel satisfied. When enough isn't enough."[2]

Although exercise addiction is a relatively newly recognized disorder, it is becoming more common. Statistics currently show that it affects at least 1 percent of the population; however, Ira Sacker, director of the Eating Disorders Program at Brookdale Medical Center in New York, estimates that about 4 percent of Americans struggle with excessive exercise. The medical information website WebMD suggests that as many as 10 percent of high-performance runners, and possibly an equal number of bodybuilders, have an exercise addiction. These exercise addicts endanger the social, emotional, and physical aspects of their lives.

Living at the Gym

As a teenager, Jason Thomas lost control over his life when he became an exercise addict. Exercise became the center of his world to the point that it was more important than his relationships with people. His addiction began when he started lifting weights to beef up his muscles. "I started off lifting 80 pounds (36.28kg), and then when I saw the muscles piling on, I started lifting more and more," he says. Eventually, Thomas was bench-pressing (lifting a barbell while lying on a bench) more than 200 pounds (91kg) and visiting the gym several times a day. "When my girlfriend complained [I was] not spending enough time with her, I felt she was making me choose between her and exercise. Exercise won."[3] Like most addicts, Thomas let his addiction control his decisions about other important parts of his life.

Also, like most addicts, Thomas did not initially realize he had a problem. He thought, like many exercise addicts, that more exercise was better. Initially excessive exercise results in positive physical results such as weight loss or more-defined muscles, so addicts continue working out, thinking that they will achieve even better results. Another reason exercise addicts

Possibly 10 percent of bodybuilders and performance runners have an exercise addiction that threatens the emotional, physical, and social aspects of their lives.

do not consider their addiction a negative act is that they often receive many compliments and praise for their appearance and for their ability to stick to an exercise routine. This feedback reinforces their belief that their habits are healthy. However, when exercise addicts continue working out for hours each day they can cause serious harm to their body, ranging from stress injuries to heart problems.

It was Thomas's mother who recognized that something was wrong with his exercise habits. She became concerned when Thomas continued working out with a fractured elbow—working out even when injured is a sign of exercise addiction. Even after being confronted with this concern, Thomas still could not stop exercising. It took treatment with a counselor to finally help Thomas deal with his addiction and develop a healthy attitude toward exercise.

Why Do People Become Addicts?

Psychologists believe that exercise addiction is typically the result of an emotional problem that is centered on a person's perception of his or her appearance. Exercise addicts often believe they have to achieve the perfect body, and their idea of perfection typically is excessive thinness (for females) or extreme muscularity (for males). This ideal look is inspired partly by the many television shows and movies starring celebrities who exemplify these body types.

For addicts, exercise is often seen as a means to the end result of achieving the ideal body. "People who overexercise usually have a distorted perception of their appearance," says Theresa Fassihi, a psychologist at the eating disorders program at the Menninger Clinic, a psychiatric facility in Houston, Texas. "They see themselves as out of shape and may become self-conscious and avoid social contact, or they may be so involved in their exercise that they don't have time for social activity."[4]

Dealing with the Problem

The good news is that, like most addictions, treatment options are available. These treatments range from counseling to admission to a treatment center that focuses on dealing with addiction. Treatment always involves discovering the core reason a person has become an addict and how the person can deal with this underlying problem.

In Thomas's case, for nearly a year he saw a therapist who specialized in eating and exercise disorders. With the help of the therapist, Thomas was able to reduce his workouts to a reasonable number where exercise again became a healthy part of his life. "I no longer feel the need to be a gym rat," he says. "I go a few times a week, work out for 45 minutes, and then get on with other things in my life."[5] Thomas realized that while exercise is a healthy habit, extreme exercise can ruin a person's life.

CHAPTER ONE

What Is Exercise Addiction?

Jessica Girdwain follows the same routine every morning. She wakes up before 5:00 A.M., runs 0.25 miles (0.4km) to the gym, and, once at the gym, she runs exactly 7.73 miles (12.4km) on the treadmill before doing twenty-five minutes of strength training exercises. Girdwain follows this up with five minutes of stretching before she walks the 0.25 miles (0.4km) home. Only on rare occasions does she allow herself to skip this routine. "I do this almost every day," she writes. "When I'm done, I complete another ritual: a mirror check to assess my lean frame and then a hop on the scale to determine my weight with painful exactitude. The result can make or break my mood for the day."[6] In addition, Girdwain walks to and from work each day, a total of 4 miles (6.4km), to ensure she is getting enough exercise.

To many, Girdwain's discipline and strict routine indicates that she is a person dedicated to health and fitness. However, several health care professionals question whether her routine is healthy physically and emotionally. While society views her excessive exercise as a positive trait, and she receives many compliments about her dedication, most physicians and psychologists believe that Girdwain's compulsion to exercise so much is an unhealthy obsession. They would classify her as an exercise addict.

Understanding Exercise

Typically, exercising is considered a positive pastime because it helps a person stay in good health. The U.S. government recommends that people exercise to stay fit and feel good about themselves both physically and mentally. It is only when people overload on exercise and significantly exceed government recommendations that exercise becomes unhealthy.

The U.S. Department of Health and Human Services (DHHS) recommends that to gain health benefits from exercise, adults should do at least 150 minutes a week of moderately intense exercise, such as swimming or walking, or 75 minutes a week of vigorously intense physical activity, such as an aerobics class or jogging. The department also recommends that in addition to cardio (heart) activity adults should do muscle-strengthening activities that involve all major muscle groups on two or more days a week. An example of someone following

General Recommendations for Physical Activity in Adults

Balance training for fall prevention

Strength training 2 to 3 times per week

Weight-bearing exercises such as walking

30 minutes or more of moderate physical activity on most, preferably all, days of the week

Taken from U.S. Department of Health & Human Services, Office of the Surgeon General, http://www.surgeongeneral.gov/library/bonehealth/chapter_7.html.

both recommendations is a person who jogs three times a week for twenty-five minutes at a time for cardio activity and also works out with free weights twice a week for strength training. Another example is a person who walks thirty minutes a day, five days a week, and works out on strength machines at a gym for twenty to thirty minutes twice a week.

"All adults can gain this health benefit of physical activity," reports the DHHS. "Age, race, and ethnicity do not matter. Men and women younger than 65 years as well as older adults have lower rates of early death when they are physically active than when they are inactive. Physically active people of all body weights (normal weight, overweight, obese) also have lower rates of early death than do inactive people."[7] Most health professionals are concerned that only 48 percent of Americans say they meet the federal recommendations for exercise.

When Is Exercise an Addiction?

On the flip side, Girdwain and other compulsive exercisers like her, concern health officials because they exercise too much. When people significantly exceed the federal recommendations of exercise without significant recovery time they may endanger themselves physically. When a person's body is not given enough time to recover from exercise, it becomes susceptible to injuries and sickness.

An exercise addict is someone who disregards injuries and other issues, such as extreme weather, that should keep them from exercising. They are obsessed with not only exercising every single day but also getting a certain amount of exercise every day, and they feel anxious and significantly guilty if they do not. Additionally, exercise addicts find themselves sacrificing their work, social aspects, and other areas of their personal lives in order to work out.

The American Psychiatric Association has not officially classified exercise addiction as a clinical disorder; however, many psychological professionals recognize exercise addiction as its own problem, resulting in health and emotional issues. According to a 2006 study, 3.6 percent of the general exercising population may be addicted to exercise.

Exercise addicts tend to disregard injuries and work out in extreme weather.

Different from Other Addictions

Unlike other addictions, exercise addiction is often termed a positive addiction. This is because most other addictions, such as to drugs, are unhealthy no matter how much or how little is consumed. With exercise, however, a moderate amount is not only good for a person, but highly recommended. It is only after the exercise becomes excessive that it becomes dangerous.

Other differences between exercise addiction and other addictions include the symptoms, or, more specifically, the lack of symptoms with exercise addiction. Often people are unaware that a person is an exercise addict because, to many, an addict's adherence to a schedule of daily exercise is considered positive and something to be praised. On the surface the behavior does not seem odd or as negatively impacting the addict's life. This is because an exercise addict can hide how excessive his or

Are You Addicted to Exercise?

Michelle Biton is a health and nutrition coach who specializes in helping people build healthy relationships with food and their bodies. She has developed thirteen causes of exercise addiction.

If you answer "yes" to one or more of these questions, you may be exercise obsessed.

1). Are you consumed with your weight or becoming fat, no matter how thin you are?

2). Is working out your number one priority?

3). Do you feel compelled to put everything else aside to exercise?

4). Does working out justify your eating?

5). Do you avoid food when you haven't done your work out?

6). Do you panic when you cannot work out?

7). Do you feel guilty when you eat?

8). Do you exercise even when you aren't feeling well, have an injury or are exhausted?

9). Do you take painkillers before a workout?

10). Do you criticize your body?

11). Do your friends and/or family comment on how much you exercise?

12). Do you need to push yourself 100 percent for every workout in order to feel like it was worthwhile?

13). Do you constantly compare yourself to others in the gym or magazines?

her exercise is by not allowing people to know exactly how much or how often he or she is exercising. For example, many exercise addicts will either wake up hours earlier than most people or stay up much later than others in order to get in the exercise they consider necessary.

An observer must look carefully to detect the signs of an exercise addict. As an example, exercise addicts will continue to work out whether or not they have an injury or a doctor has recommended that they rest. Additionally, addicts will continue their exercise program no matter what the weather, even if it means running through snow in below-freezing temperatures or through excessive heat that can cause sunstroke. Lastly, exercise addicts will start to avoid social functions or even their jobs in order to get in their "required" exercise.

Disrupted Lives

Compulsive exercisers have extreme trouble living a normal life as exercise becomes more and more the center of their lives. Elizabeth B. Krieger, a recovered exercise addict, would work out four or more hours a day when she was in college, resulting in both her academic and social life suffering. Although she realized this was happening, she could not stop herself. "I made it to my 'Archaeology of Death' class only half the time because it conflicted with the open swim hours at the pool. I would cancel on friends to accommodate my workouts, or not even make plans with them at all," Krieger writes. "With so many athletic outlets to choose from, I chose them all, from aerobics (step, hi-low) to weights to running—my bread and butter, if you will. I was already playing varsity lacrosse (until I got cut from the team), but I'd still preface the grueling two-and-a-half-hour practices with my own six-mile run."[8]

Exercise addicts such as Krieger experience withdrawal and feel a psychological and/or physiological dependence on their regular exercise program. Typically, after twenty-four to thirty-six hours of no exercise, an addict experiences withdrawal symptoms. These symptoms may include anxiety, irritability, nervousness, and guilt even if the circumstances that kept them from exercising were beyond their control. "Many compulsive exercisers have behaviors similar to drug addicts. The athlete no longer finds pleasure in exercise, but feels it is necessary. It is no longer a choice; it has become an obligation," writes Elizabeth Quinn, an exercise physiologist and fitness consultant. "While exercise may provide a temporary feeling of well-being or euphoria, the athlete requires more and more exercise to reach this state. If he is forced to miss a workout, he will report overwhelming feelings of guilt and anxiety, similar to withdrawal symptoms."[9]

Physical Symptoms

Initially, a compulsive exerciser sees positive results through muscle gain, cardio endurance, and flexibility; however, when a person pushes the body to the point of injury and exhaustion, the body begins to rebel, and the initial positive results are negated by injuries and stress. At this point, compulsive exercisers will begin to exhibit the physical symptoms of their exercising. For example, although moderate amounts of exercise strengthen the immune system, which makes people less prone to illness, too much exercise has the opposite effect. A compulsive exerciser is likely to experience fatigue, lethargy, and dizziness and is more likely to contract an illness due to a weakened immune system. Additionally a person who exercises excessively may develop an elevated heart rate even when resting and may also experience insomnia.

Compulsive exercising also causes painful injuries, including stress fractures, damaged bones and joints, and torn muscles, ligaments, and tendons. The reason for the physical symptoms is that compulsive exercisers expose their bodies to excessive stress over long periods of time without giving their bodies time to rest and repair themselves. "When an individual feels pain, the body is literally communicating that something is wrong. If the symptom is ignored, it tends to worsen. Individuals who experience overuse injuries usually ignore, deny or mislabel their body signals," write Pauline Powers and Ron Thompson, authors of *Exercise Balance*. "Whatever the cause of the stress fracture, when the activity is continued, the damage gets worse."[10]

Compulsive exercisers are likely to experience fatigue, lethargy, and dizziness and are more likely to contract illness due to a weakened immune system.

Causes of Exercise Addiction

What would make a person exercise to beyond injury? Most health professionals believe the causes of exercise addiction are psychological and that the primary psychological cause is that an exercise addict has a poor body image. For those who become addicts due to body image, their exercise addiction is a way to achieve what they believe to be the perfect body, which is typically excessive thinness for females and either a lean and slender or bulky and muscular body for males.

Another psychological reason for overexercising is that addicts use it as a way to gain control over their lives. Often these types of people are perfectionists who want order in all aspects of their lives but often find exercise to be the only area that they can control.

Nigel is an example of a person who suffered from excessive exercise and anorexia for years as a way to maintain some control in his life. He experienced exercise addiction and anorexia whenever he dealt with stress and difficult issues in his life. "I have on occasions got up at 3 am to go for a run because I knew I would be working a long shift but HAD to exercise,"

What Is a Behavioral Addiction?

When most people think of addiction they think of drugs and alcohol; however, people can become addicted to types of behavior, such as gambling, using the Internet, and exercising. These types of addictions typically are considered behavioral, when a person has a recurring compulsion to engage in some specific activity despite any negative impacts on the person's health, mental state, or social life. The health profession has only recently studied behavioral addictions, but early research has found that symptoms are similar to substance addiction. "When an individual is unable to control or stop an activity, despite experiencing adverse consequences of the activity, that person is a behavioral addict," writes Mike Bayer, chief executive officer of Treatment4addiction.com. "It's as though there is an invisible line [crossed, after] which a person has lost the ability to choose. For example, [for shopaholics,] they no longer want to shop, but they need to continue to shop to regulate brain chemistry. Very often such a person knows that his impulse is misplaced, wants to stop, but is unable to do so. It is this loss of control that is most characteristic of addiction."

Mike Bayer, "Most Common Forms of Psychological Dependency," Treatment4addiction.com, February 2009. www.treatment4addiction.com/addiction/behavioral.

People can become addicted to particular types of behaviors, such as online gambling or the Internet.

Nigel writes. "Not only that but my work was very active, and once again I cycled to and from work with the return journey including a long and steep climb. There were times I've been for a run in agony due to an injury, but ignored it because I HAD to exercise to be able to eat. There were other occasions where I was so tired I was barely capable of running any further due to no energy and feeling faint."[11]

Adding to these psychological issues is the positive reinforcement exercise addicts often receive from friends and family. Because exercise is normally a healthy habit, when not done to excess, it is hard to see when a person has gone too far. Instead, addicts often receive compliments about their physique and dedication to fitness. These compliments encourage addicts to continue with their obsession and allow them to think their obsession is normal and acceptable.

Physical Addiction

New research shows that exercise may also be physically addictive, which could contribute to a person's becoming a compulsive exerciser. The body releases endorphins when a person exercises for a certain amount of time. Endorphins are brain chemicals that give people a sense of euphoria, otherwise known as a "high."

Discovered in 1975, endorphins are believed to reduce and relieve pain, enhance the immune system, and reduce stress. The amount of exercise it takes for the brain to release endorphins depends on the person's body. For some, endorphins may be released after jogging for only ten minutes while others will jog for half an hour before this occurs. Research has shown that the more physically fit an athlete is, the more receptive the athlete's body is to released endorphins. Additionally, as the intensity and duration of an athlete's exercise increases, the amount of endorphins released also increases. "Exercise is a powerful drug. It seduces many with its zen-like state, a feeling that was fondly coined the "runner's high" in the 1970s. The lure of exercise is often so strong that it can turn enthusiasts into addicts,"[12] writes K. Cossaboon, a fitness writer with Hub Pages, a website dedicated to providing up-to-date information on all topics.

In addition to obtaining a physical high from exercise, addicts may also experience physical withdrawal symptoms. This is based on research at Boston's Tufts University that shows rats that exercise experience withdrawal symptoms when they are forced to stop. According to a 2009 report of their findings, scientists at Tufts studied rats that were split into two groups, with one group given exercise wheels and the other remaining inactive. Rats were chosen for the experiment because a rat's nervous system is similar to a human's, according to the researchers.

In order to observe immediate withdrawal symptoms in the exercise-addicted rats, researchers gave all the rats naloxone, a drug administered to heroin addicts in order to counteract overdose and to produce immediate withdrawal. Of the active and inactive rats, the active rats displayed more withdrawal symptoms than the inactive ones. A rat that ran excessively experienced severe withdrawal symptoms, according to the researchers. These symptoms included trembling, writhing, teeth chattering, and drooping eyelids, which are similar symptoms heroin addicts experience while going through withdrawal. According to the report, "Because of the way the active rats responded to naloxone, they seemed to have undergone the same changes in the brain's reward system as rats addicted to drugs. Exercise, like drugs of abuse, leads to the release of neurotransmitters such as endorphins and dopamine, which are involved with a sense of reward."[13]

Diagnosis

Because exercising is considered an admirable activity, it is hard to diagnose if a person is overexercising to the point of addiction. For example, a person who exercises for hours at a time while ignoring injury and exhaustion might be an exercise addict or he might simply be overtraining. Athletes are susceptible to overtraining syndrome, which is when a person has been intensively training and stressing the body without giving it adequate time to recover and rest between training periods. This might occur when athletes are intensely training for upcoming events.

The difference between an athlete who excessively exercises and one who does not is that the non-addict realizes when he is overtraining and needs to take a break.

The difference between athletes and addicts is that athletes will recognize that they are overtraining and will take a break, while addicts will continue to push their bodies to unsafe levels. Athletes realize that the body only gets stronger and improves in performance when there are adequate rest periods following hard training. An exercise addict will ignore the symptoms and continue on with his or her exercise because performance is not their ultimate goal—completing the "required" exercises is.

If overtraining is ruled out and the person is exhibiting compulsive exercise symptoms, then it is likely the person is addicted. Before addicts can get help, they must come to that realization themselves. If exercise addicts suspect something is wrong with them, they can look at exercise addiction criteria that have been developed to help them diagnose themselves.

Self-Realization

It took Jenny Moran several years before she realized that she was addicted to exercise. At age thirty, she started running for the simple reason of wanting to get in better shape. Initially, that is what happened as she gained control of her weight and felt in great shape. But over the next few years running became the center of her life.

For an exercise addict, running can become a full-time obsession.

Moran's workouts became an everyday obligation, more important than nearly anything else in her life. It got to the point that she specifically ran in order to burn off the calories she had eaten in the day. "Running consumed my thoughts," Moran, now forty-two, says. "Every day I sat at work thinking about running. It was like a crazy voice in my head. That's when I knew something was really wrong."[14]

Once Moran realized how obsessed she had become, she began on the road to recovery. Today she works out, but exercise does not control her life. "I think that running has given me lots of positive things," she says, "but I also think that it's an easy place to hide out if you have a problem; it can be hard to imagine the negative side of it."[15]

Like Moran, Jessica Girdwain also realized the negative side of compulsive exercise and has been able to start changing her lifestyle and attitude toward exercise. She continues to exercise but is more likely to take time off and not be as stringent about her routines so that she does not damage her physical and emotional well-being. Both Moran and Girdwain had to recognize their addiction and its implications before they could work toward recovery.

CHAPTER TWO

Exercise Addiction Is Tied to Other Disorders

Exercise addiction is a problem on its own, but it can also be tied to several other psychological disorders. Most commonly, exercise addiction is linked to eating disorders such as anorexia and bulimia, but it has also been associated with obsessive-compulsive disorder and body dysmorphic disorder. In such cases, exercise addiction is often just a symptom of the psychological disorder.

Anorexia

Eating disorders are the most common disorders that exercise addiction is linked to. This is because eating disorders are often centered on a person's body image and the need for control in their lives. People with eating disorders, such as anorexia, may not only use food but also exercise as a way of controlling calories and weight. "They focus on controlling their bodies because they feel they can't control anything else in their lives,"[16] says Susie Mendelsohn, a Blue Ash, Ohio, clinical psychologist and former eating disorder sufferer.

Anorexia nervosa, or simply "anorexia," is one of the most common eating disorders. People with anorexia, called anorexics, have a great fear of gaining weight. Anorexics constantly think about food and how to limit what food they eat, even when

Exercise addiction can be linked to anorexia and other eating disorders.

Narcissism and Overexercise

Exercise addiction can be a symptom of a less common psychological disorder known as narcissistic personality disorder. According to the Mayo Clinic, "Narcissistic personality disorder is a mental disorder in which people have an inflated sense of their own importance and a deep need for admiration. Those with narcissistic personality disorder believe that they are superior to others and have little regard for other people's feelings." Exercise addiction can be a part of narcissistic personality disorder when a person considers his or her body better than all others. He or she becomes entirely self-absorbed with exercise as a way to remain in what he or she considers perfect condition. This can happen because underneath all of the narcissistic behavior is extremely low self-esteem. People with this disorder have a secret fear of humiliation and shame so, in the case of those who consider their bodies perfect, they will do everything they can, including compulsive exercising, in order to maintain their ideal body.

Mayo Clinic, "Narcissistic Personality Disorder," November 19, 2009. www.mayo clinic.com/ health/narcissistic-personality-disorder/DS00652.

Narcissistic personality disorder gives people an inflated sense of their own importance and deep need to be admired. Exercise addiction can be a symptom of this disorder.

they are too thin. Anorexia is a way of limiting food intake in order to gain control of one's life or to ease tension, anger, and anxiety.

Anorexia affects about 1 in 1000 people, equating to 272,000 people in the United States. Approximately 90 to 95 percent of anorexics are women. According to the National Institute of Mental Health, anorexia affects a total of 0.5 to 3.7 percent of females.

The most common symptom of anorexia is weighing much less than is healthy or normal and attempting to hide this from others. Anorexics are afraid to gain any weight and think that they are overweight even if they are very thin. Other symptoms include strictly limiting how much they eat, such as only allowing themselves a few hundred calories a day instead of the two thousand or so typically recommended. Additionally, anorexics often will refuse certain foods, such as those high in fat or sugar. They may develop strange food habits such as chewing their food a certain number of times or cutting up their food into tiny bites.

The dangers of anorexia are great. According to Anorexia Nervosa and Related Eating Disorders, Inc., without treatment, up to 20 percent of people with serious eating disorders die. Even with treatment, 2 to 3 percent of people with anorexia die due to the damage they have already done to their bodies. Anorexia mortality rates are the highest of any psychological disorder because when the body is starved, it can develop potentially fatal medical conditions. These conditions include heart disease, kidney and liver disease, and potassium and magnesium imbalances that can lead to heart failure. Other physical issues that can result are osteoporosis, low blood pressure, ulcers, dizziness and fainting, irregular heart rhythms, headaches, and nausea.

Anorexia and Compulsive Exercise

Of those with anorexia, approximately 80 percent also engage in compulsive exercise. Those who experience both anorexia and exercise addiction have what is termed *anorexia athletica*. Anorexia athletica compounds the potential dangers of anorexia nervosa. Anorexics are already starving their bodies, and when they exercise excessively, they burn even more calories. This exhausts the body's already weakened resources, and an increased chance of fractures and even heart conditions is possible.

Michelle Trotta has endured anorexia and exercise addiction for more than thirty years. Trotta has starved herself and overexercised in order to attain a zero dress size. Her quest has resulted in harm both physically and emotionally. "I've lost three-fourths of my teeth. I've fractured my tailbone three times. I have crutches in my house, and I don't think there's a day where I don't have some kind of pain," says Trotta. "But it still doesn't stop me."[17]

Trotta has the symptoms of both an anorexic and an exercise addict. As an anorexic she calculates every last calorie she eats and forbids herself many foods. For example, every year at Christmas she bakes fifteen hundred cookies yet forbids herself to eat any. As an exercise addict she runs 5 miles (8km) every day, which itself is not excessive, but what is obsessive is that she will run at 11:00 P.M. if she failed to run earlier, and she will run no matter how poorly her body feels.

Bulimia

Exercise addiction is also associated with bulimia, another eating disorder. Bulimia is a psychological disorder in which a person will binge on food even though he or she knows it is unhealthy. A bulimic will then use vomiting, laxatives, diuretics, or a combination of these to get rid of the calories in order to avoid weight gain. Estimates show that one-third of people struggling with bulimia use laxatives, while approximately 10 percent take diuretics. The others purge through vomiting or exercise.

When bingeing and purging, the bulimic experiences a loss of control that is followed by a short-lived calmness and then followed by self-loathing. This cycle becomes compulsive and is constantly repeated. A 2007 study based on the National Institute of Mental Health–funded National Comorbidity Survey Replication (NCS-R) found that 1.5 percent of women and 0.5

Bulimics binge and then use vomiting or laxatives to prevent any weight gain.

Often a person's obsession with his or her body being "perfect" results in bulimia and exercise addiction disorders.

percent of men reported having bulimia and enduring these cycles. The same study found that people with bulimia typically had endured the condition for eight years.

Bulimics are typically aware that their bingeing and purging is abnormal and, as a result, hide their actions from others. Because of this, they often experience great fear and guilt after bingeing and purging. Despite these feelings they are compelled to continue the cycle. The exact cause of this compulsion is unknown, but psychologists believe it is related to various emotional issues such as trauma, family problems, or poor self-esteem or body image. Binge eating is often a response to depression, stress, or self-esteem issues. "Although the overt symptoms of bulimia revolve around food behaviors and a fear of gaining weight, bulimia is actually a way to cope with personal distress and emotional pain," writes Lindsey Hall and Leigh Cohn, authors of *Bulimia: A Guide to Recovery.* "Eating binges take time and focus away from more disturbing issues, and purges are an effective way to regain the control and feelings of safety lost during the binge."[18]

Serious medical problems can result after a prolonged period of bingeing and purging. Frequent vomiting brings stomach acid into the esophagus, which can permanently damage it. Because of purging, a bulimic's tooth enamel starts to wear away due to the stomach acids in the mouth. A bulimic's hair, skin, and nails become dry and unhealthy, and bulimics often endure constant stomachaches and diarrhea. Additionally, the immune system of a bulimic weakens, which makes him or her susceptible to illness.

Bulimia and Exercise Addiction

Many with bulimia also suffer from exercise addiction. Instead of, or sometimes in addition to, purging, persons with exercise addiction and bulimia use exercise as a way to rid themselves of calories that they take in when bingeing. Approximately 55 percent of patients with bulimia also compulsively exercise.

Compulsive exercise compounds bulimia's problems because the excessive exercise further strains the body and depletes it of needed calories and nutrients. In addition to bulimia's typical dangers, bulimics who excessively exercise are at greater risk for sprains, broken bones, and a weakened immune system. The depletion of calories and nutrients also leads to greater risk for heart problems, which can be fatal.

Jessica Setnick's obsession with her body and being "perfect" resulted in her developing bulimia and exercise addiction. Setnick became obsessed with getting the perfect body because she was unable to achieve perfection in other areas of her life, such as achieving a 4.0 average in college. Her need for perfection manifested itself in her quest to have the perfect body.

Initially Setnick binged and purged but then realized she could also exercise to rid herself of calories. In addition to bingeing and purging she started to log nearly fifty hours of exercise a week. She was able to hide this behavior because she worked at a fitness center. After a while, Setnick finally realized that the bingeing, purging, and exercise routine was not achieving what she considered a perfect body; instead her body was revolting to her, and she was becoming sick and exhausted. "The moment I realized that 'perfect' wasn't all it was cracked up to be, I was kneeling on the carpeted floor of my mother's bathroom. The remains of my dinner bobbed in the toilet basin, a floating testament to my dedication, determination, and sheer willpower. Here was proof that I could do whatever it took to be, well, perfect. But as I leaned against the wall, reality closed in around me. This was perfect? Swollen, bloodshot eyes. A throat so inflamed it was difficult to swallow. My self-esteem in tatters," writes Setnick.

> Where just moments before, I'd felt relief—pride, even—suddenly there was only despair. Sitting there, wasted from the effort of forcing myself to vomit for the umpteenth time that week, I was tired of doing this. Tired of hating myself that much. That night was the beginning of the end of my battle with bulimia.[19]

Setnick went on to beat her bulimia and exercise addiction and become a dietician who helps others with similar problems.

The Flip Side

Although excessive exercise can be a symptom of obsessive-compulsive disorder (OCD), it can also be part of this disorder's treatment. In cases where OCD is predominated by other rituals, such as hand washing or counting, counselors have found that exercise can actually help alleviate a patient's symptoms. A 2007 hospital study found that aerobic exercise was helpful in reducing the severity of OCD symptoms. In the study, fifteen participants continued with their usual OCD treatment but also added moderate-intensity aerobic exercise to their treatment schedule for twelve weeks. Researchers found that both the severity and frequency of OCD symptoms were reduced right after exercise and over the entire twelve-week period. The key to relieving the symptoms was moderate, not excessive, exercise.

OCD sufferers often engage in repetitive behaviors, such as compulsively washing their hands. Exercise can alleviate the symptoms of the disorder.

Obsessive-Compulsive Disorder

Another psychological problem that exercise addiction can be associated with is obsessive-compulsive disorder, or OCD. OCD is an anxiety disorder that is characterized by recurring thoughts and repetitive behaviors that a person feels compelled to perform. Examples of such behaviors include frequent hand washing, counting, and cleaning. These behaviors are done a certain way and a certain number of times and, to the person with OCD, these rituals cannot vary.

When people with OCD perform these behaviors it is with the hope that they will prevent obsessive thoughts; however, these rituals only provide temporary relief, and not performing them markedly increases anxiety. This cycle can take up hours of a person's day and interfere with normal activities. Often people with OCD know that their obsessions and compulsions are a problem but they cannot stop themselves.

About 2.3 percent of the population between the ages of eighteen and fifty-four suffer from OCD, which is a greater number than suffer from other mental disorders, such as schizophrenia, bipolar disorder, or panic disorder. In the United States, approximately 3.3 million people have OCD, equating to around 1 percent of the country's children and 2 percent of its adults.

Although OCD does not usually result in physical problems, it can severely disrupt a person's life. Because of the amount of time required to devote to rituals, someone suffering from OCD may not be able to live his or her life fully and may not have normal relationships with others.

Compulsive Exercise

Exercise addiction can be a symptom of OCD. As opposed to pure exercise addiction, where people exercise excessively in order to maintain what they consider a "perfect" body or as an extreme way to deal with stress, exercise addiction as an OCD symptom occurs when people use exercise as their compulsive ritual to rid themselves of their obsessive thoughts. "Exercise addiction might also be a symptom of obsessive-compulsive disorder if the exercise is intended to relieve feelings of anxiety about some feared consequence other than weight gain,"[20] write Hollyann E. Jenkins and clinical psychologist Monnica Williams.

People with OCD compulsively exercise to rid themselves of obsessive thoughts, such as that they are overweight. The constant exercising to rid themselves of these thoughts parallel OCD patients who feel they must wash their hands a certain number of times each day in order to rid themselves of germs.

The physical dangers of a person with OCD and exercise addiction are that they can exhaust their bodies, weaken their hearts, overstress their ligaments and bones, and weaken their immune systems. Emotionally, they harm themselves because their minds cannot get rid of thoughts of exercise, and they experience intense guilt and depression if they do not perform their routines.

Cindee, who was featured on cable channel A&E's program *Obsessed*, is an example of someone who experiences obsessive-compulsive disorder in the form of exercise. Cindee feels she must exercise every single day for three hours at a time. She owns several types of exercise equipment, including two treadmills, free weights, and ankle weights, in addition to being a member of a gym. She has not missed a day of working out for the past fifteen years other than to give birth. The last time Cindee's workout schedule changed was when her treadmill broke in the middle of her workout. She could not wait to get it fixed so she bought another treadmill the same day in order to complete her "set" amount of workout time.

On the show, when Cindee is told to stop her exercise after only a half hour on the treadmill, her disorder becomes apparent—she is upset and shows obvious anxiety. She experiences dry mouth, a churning stomach, and rambling thoughts. When asked what she is thinking, Cindee says, "I need to go more, and I can't. Somebody's stopping me, and it kinda [ticks] me off. . . . It's like I can't focus. My heart's beating; I can't control my hand."[21] Her obsessive compulsive disorder disrupts both her health and relationships, but she cannot stop herself.

Body Dysmorphic Disorder

Another mental disorder to which exercise addiction can be linked is body dysmorphic disorder, a mental disorder that makes

Exercise addiction is linked to body dysmorphic disorder, a mental disorder that gives people a distorted view of their body.

a person constantly worry about a flaw, either real or imagined, with how they look. The flaw upsets such people so much that they do not want others to see them. They obsess constantly about their "flaw" and what they can do to fix it. The most common concern people with body dysmorphic disorder have is with their skin—for example, acne or scarring—which occurs in about 75 percent of patients. Many are fixated on their hair or nose while others worry about their weight, thighs, teeth, or face. The body part a person focuses on may change over time.

Approximately 1 percent of the population suffers from body dysmorphic disorder. The disorder usually begins in adolescence, but is often not diagnosed or treated until a decade or more later when it becomes more severe and the symptoms become more apparent to others. Men and women are equally likely to develop body dysmorphic disorder.

Typical symptoms displayed by sufferers include being preoccupied with their physical appearance and, as a result, constantly examining themselves in the mirror or actively avoiding mirrors. They may also excessively groom themselves, such as constantly plucking eyebrows or wearing extreme amounts of makeup. Other signs include refusing to appear in pictures and avoiding being in social situations. "Individuals with body dysmorphic disorder are often full of shame and hide from others," says Pam Kasinetz, a psychotherapist and clinical manager of outpatient services at Thomas Jefferson University's Department of Psychiatry and Human Behavior in Philadelphia.

> They engage in ritualistic behaviors in an attempt to hide the perceived flaw. There is both a preoccupation [with] and avoidance of mirrors. People with body dysmorphic disorder often seek dermatological or cosmetic surgical procedures yet do not gain satisfaction from these. And there is a constant need for reassurance by others about the perceived deficit and an avoidance of social situations due to extreme self-consciousness about their appearance.[22]

Often people with body dysmorphic disorder go to extreme measures to try to fix their perceived flaws. For example, a woman unhappy with her face may undergo excessive cosmetic surgery procedures. Another who dislikes her body may try extreme diets and even starvation to lose weight.

Excessive Exercise to "Fix" the Flaw

Compulsive exercise is one way that people with body dysmorphic disorder try to fix what they consider flaws. For women, this is often when they think their bodies are too heavy and then engage in excessive exercise in order to lose weight. For men, body dysmorphic disorder often makes them feel that their muscles are too small and so they compulsively exercise in order to bulk up. This subset of body dysmorphic disorder is known as muscle dysmorphia.

Muscle dysmorphia normally leads men to excercise excessively and to use dietary supplements or even steroids to increase their overall shape and muscle tone. For years Michael Feldman suffered from eating disorders and muscle dysmorphia. His battle began with anorexia but then turned into muscle dysmorphia. "After seeing a picture of myself and thinking I was way too 'skinny' and 'scrawny,' I flipped and became muscle dysmorphic—where I thought I was too small and constantly worked out to achieve a bigger body,"[23] says Feldman, an actor and performer. Feldman eventually created *Muscle-Bound,* a multimedia solo performance combined with an original film documentary that centers on male body-image issues, including eating disorders, steroid-abuse, and gym culture.

The dangers of body dysmorphic disorder combined with exercise addiction are both psychological and physical. According to a hospital study, about 80 percent of people with body dysmorphic disorder consider suicide, and about 25 percent of people with the disorder have attempted suicide. Physically, people with body dysmorphic disorder who excessively exercise endanger themselves by exhausting themselves, weakening their immune systems, and weakening their bones and muscles.

In all cases, excessive exercise compounds the problems of other psychological disorders. Whether a person is diagnosed with an exercise addiction as his or her primary problem or as a symptom of another disorder, the dangers can be severe. Unless the person gets some form of help, his or her physical and emotional health will suffer.

CHAPTER THREE

Who Is Most at Risk for Exercise Addiction?

People with certain characteristics are more at risk for becoming exercise addicts than others. Generally, people with low self-esteem, who are unhappy with their bodies and who seek perfection and control in all areas of their lives, or are high performers, such as athletes, are at the greatest risk for letting exercise become the center of their lives, prohibiting a normal existence.

One of the most common types of people to become addicted to exercise is the high-performing athlete. Athletes lend themselves to exercise addiction because of the already prominent part exercise plays in their lives. Although many athletes are able to endure long workouts on a regular basis and not become addicts, other athletes prone to addiction cross the line from intense training to exercise addiction.

The difference between intensely exercising and being an exercise addict is that the exercise addict will not stop exercising even when a trainer or doctor tells him or her that exercise is taking over his or her normal life. "Exercise addiction is not just another term for overtraining syndrome," states the American Running Association. The association notes,

Healthy athletes training for peak performance and competition can suffer overtraining symptoms, which are the short-term result of too little rest and recovery. Exercise addiction, on the other hand, is a chronic loss of perspective of the role of exercise in a full life. A healthy athlete and an exercise addict may share similar levels of training volume—the difference is in the attitude.[24]

According to WebMD, as many as 10 percent of high-performance runners, and possibly an equal number of bodybuilders, have an exercise addiction. It initially develops because athletes yearn to become the best they can be, but soon the addiction becomes even more important than the athletic performance. They will train to the point that their body is exhausted or physically damaged, negating all positive training results, and they cannot stop because of their compulsion.

Extreme Races

Athletes who participate in so-called ultra, or extreme, races in which they run for up to 100 miles (161km) and in severe climates, such as the extreme cold of Antarctica or the baking heat of Death Valley, are among those more likely to become addicted to exercise. This is because many who enter these races are perfectionists who want to be the best at their sport, and because ultra racing is such an intense sport, exercise becomes the center of their lives in their quest for perfection.

Stan Jensen understands firsthand the addictive qualities of ultra running. Jensen has competed in 20 marathons and 125 ultramarathons in his lifetime. He admits that his sport is attractive to athletes with addictive personalities. "I . . . know people in my sport who are former alcoholics, or heroin addicts. They say 'you know, I have a problem with addiction, but this is the healthiest addiction I can have,'"[25] said Jensen.

Other extreme racing sports include triathlons and the Ironman competition. Michele Wallace, a columnist who writes about training for triathlons, believes that those who participate in extreme races are at risk for exercise addiction. Specifically, she cites the Ironman, a 2.4-mile (3.9km) swim, 112-mile (180km) bike race, and 26.2-mile (42km) run, as a cause for compulsive exercise and training. "Those that cross the finish line and hear those words 'You are an Ironman' are congratulated

High-performance athletes who participate in ultra races are more likely to become addicted to exercise than others.

and revered for their dedication, strength and fortitude. Prior to crossing this finish line, however, what were the sacrifices made?" writes Wallace. "What lies in the depths of the road they traveled to get to that finish line? For some, the journey is constructive, for others the journey is damaging—for everyone, the journey is extreme."[26]

Perceived Bodies

Young women are among the groups of people most at risk for exercise addiction. According to a 2009 study by the University of Delaware, teenage girls perceive themselves as being more than 10 pounds (4.5kg) heavier than they actually are. For their study, researchers asked 172 adolescents (aged thirteen to seventeen) to pick one of twenty-seven silhouettes that resembled how they saw themselves and then to pick another silhouette that matched their ideal weight. The study results showed that the girls on average viewed themselves as weighing 141 pounds (64kg), which was 8 pounds (3.6kg) more than their average weight (133 pounds/60.5kg) and 11 pounds (5kg) more than their ideal weight (130 pounds/59kg).

Studies have shown that teenage girls perceive themselves as 10 pounds heavier than they really are.

One Coach's Experience

Former athletes are susceptible to exercise addiction because so much of their lives had revolved around being competitive athletically that, even when they are no longer athletes, they continue to keep the mindset of wanting to be the best and most competitive physically. Girls' basketball coach Lindsay Adcock of Cherokee Trail High School in Aurora, Colorado, became an exercise addict and suffered from eating disorders after her college athletic career ended. Adcock's exercise addiction began in her athletic years.

Adcock played basketball until her senior year in college; much of her identity was linked to being competitive, athletic, and part of a team. When she no longer competed, Adcock felt a void in her life and decided to continue to train as an athlete. This training, however, quickly led to an unhealthy addiction. Adcock started training for a half marathon, switching from being a team athlete to a solitary one. She discovered she enjoyed running long distances because it kept her occupied and relaxed, in addition to helping her maintain what she considered a good weight with muscle tone. When she was not running, however, she was lonely and missed the friendship of teammates.

To deal with loneliness, Adcock increased her daily exercise routine and also started walking to classes, often forcing herself to walk faster or walk on her toes to engage her calf muscles and therefore burn more calories. Soon she was working out strenuously for four to five hours a day, before, between, and after classes. Her whole world centered on her workouts to the extent that she gave up time with her husband and family to keep up her exercise routine.

It took years for Adcock to realize the effect her exercise addiction and eating disorder were having on her life. "An eating disorder makes you the most selfish person," she says. "I'm going through a divorce because of this. My husband says that I didn't give him enough attention because I was so focused on myself."[27] Adcock suffered liver damage and arthritis and was eventually hospitalized due to these and other problems that resulted from bulimia and overexercise. She entered an eating disorder program and is finally getting her normal life back.

High Achievers

Like current and former athletes, high achievers and perfectionists are at greater risk than others for becoming obsessed with exercise. Often when they cannot achieve the levels they want in other areas of their lives, perfectionists turn to exercise because it is something they can control. As a result, high achievers may become obsessed with exercise, constantly adding more time and difficulty to their exercise routines. "Intense, high-achieving perfectionist individuals are particularly vulnerable to this addiction,"[28] says psychologist Sharon Stoliaroff.

Angela Liddon, a self-professed high achiever in all areas of her life, became focused on exercise when she started training to complete a half marathon. Her need for accomplishment soon turned her training into an exercise addiction. Her workouts increased from a daily run to a daily run followed by intense DVD-led workouts and nightly yoga. Additionally, during each run she would give herself a 2-mile (3.2km) army test during which she would run as fast as she could and time herself. "It's the superwoman syndrome," says Liddon. "I felt I had to do it all to perform well."[29]

The problem is that an exercise addiction eventually results in a person hurting himself or herself physically, sometimes chronically. Liddon ended up in the emergency room with a pelvic injury due to her excessive exercise. As a result, she could not exercise for months, and this finally forced her to gain perspective on establishing limits for her body.

Body Image Issues

Another group of people particularly susceptible to exercise addiction is young women with body-image issues. These women are particularly affected by the proliferation of thin, beautiful, and athletic women featured in advertisements for beauty products and clothes, in fashion shows, and in movies and television programs. Because the body size of female models and celebrities tends to be significantly smaller than the average woman's, this ideal can affect how impressionable young women view themselves.

The average American woman is 5 feet 4 (1.625m) and weighs 140 pounds (64kg). The average American female model is 5 feet 11 (1.8m) and weighs 117 pounds (53kg).

According to the National Eating Disorders Association, the average American woman is 5 feet, 4 inches (162.5cm) tall and weighs 140 pounds (64kg). The average American model is 5 feet, 11 inches (1.8m) tall and weighs 117 pounds (53kg). This dramatic difference in body size can affect the average woman's self-image. As a result, young women with poor self-images may turn to extreme exercise or other related disorders, such as bulimia or anorexia, in order to lose weight and look more like a model.

As a fourteen-year-old, Jessica Weiner was definitely affected by what she considered the world's view of the perfect body. To get this body, she began an extreme exercise routine in order to work off every calorie she ate. She would work out four to six hours a day, waking up early and going to the gym, then returning there after school. "I became withdrawn and isolated," she says. "And I was very focused on my appearance. I was hypercritical of myself and had drastic mood shifts."[30]

Weiner's exercise addiction worsened to the point that she panicked if she could not get her workout in. One day when she was seventeen, she realized she would not be able to meet her daily exercise routine. Because she could not work out and burn calories, she decided to make herself throw up; however, just before she was about to throw up, Weiner stopped herself and realized she had a problem. Since then, she has gotten therapy and counseling and developed a healthier viewpoint of herself, food, and exercise. In her twenties she toured the United States, performing her play, *Body Loathing, Body Love*, which centers on her struggle with exercise.

A New Group

Young women are not the only ones affected by society's perception of the perfect body. Today young men are also being bombarded with media and entertainment messages that emphasize fit male bodies. As a result, they are also at risk of exercise addiction and related body-image disorders.

According to Dr. Theodore Weltzin, medical director of the eating disorder programs at Rogers Memorial Hospital in Oconomowoc, Wisconsin, male patients' exercise addiction is normally not focused on losing weight but on developing upper body strength. The drive for this, he believes, is a desire to achieve the muscular male body type seen in advertisements, movies, television, and other popular media.

Winchester University psychologist David Giles conducted a study that found exercise addiction to be prevalent in males who read men's magazines such as *Men's Health*. These men end up aspiring to get the physique of the magazines' male models. "We found that the more such magazines a man reads, the more likely he is to be anxious about his physique,"[31] says Giles. Together with his coauthor, Jessica Close, Giles interviewed 161 men aged between eighteen and thirty-six and

A Winchester University study found that exercise addiction in males is closely linked to reading men's magazines such as *Men's Health*, whereby some men aspire to obtain the "perfect" physiques of the magazines' male models.

asked them which male magazines they read, and for how long. They also assessed the men's diets, how much they exercised, and how they felt about their looks. According to Giles, these magazines make men anxious about their appearance and lead to excessive means to try to attain the ideal body.

Not only do magazines and other media make men anxious about their physiques, but even today's toys impact how men perceive themselves. In the last several decades, images of the ideal male body have grown increasingly more muscular and, according to a recent study of the muscularity of action-figure toys past and present, today's action-figure toys show more muscular men. Scaled to human dimensions, the original 1965 G.I. Joe would have a biceps circumference of about 11 inches (28cm)—similar to an ordinary man, but the 1995 G.I. Joe Extreme would have 26-inch (66cm) biceps—larger than any bodybuilder in history.

The greater focus on a muscular physique results in men developing a greater chance of becoming exercise addicts. Particularly affected are male bodybuilders, whose goal is to attain the ideal body. Jack Haber, a personal trainer and champion bodybuilder, became addicted to weight lifting. "It grew, the addiction grew and grew," Haber said. "It was a reverse anorexia. Because I had a fear of regressing, of losing the size that I had built [up]."[32] Haber says that his whole world became weight lifting, and his focus was solely on keeping what he considered the perfect body.

More Male Issues

Men who are more concerned with being thin than muscular become exercise addicts who are obsessed with losing weight, excessively exercising to burn off calories. For example, Weltzin of Rogers Memorial Hospital, had a forty-five-year-old male patient who believed he had to exercise any time he ate. This man had been teased about his weight as a child and, as a result, developed an emotional need to exercise to rid himself of calories.

Author Gary Grahl wrote about his own personal struggle with anorexia and exercise addiction in his book *Skinny Boy*.

Men who were teased about their weight as children can sometimes develop an exercise addiction.

Grahl grew up in a small town in Wisconsin and always set high expectations for himself. As a freshman in high school, he was the starting quarterback, kicker, punter, running back, and defensive back on the freshman football team and the starting point guard on the basketball team. Additionally, he was friendly with everyone, feeling a need to please all around him.

His need for perfection in all areas of his life led him to become obsessed with exercise routines and keeping an extremely low weight. "I'd wake up at 3:30 A.M. to exercise for three to four hours a day, then again after school. I was an All-American boy trying to achieve,"[33] he explains. Grahl was eventually hospitalized six times over a five-year period for anorexia nervosa and depression and finally recovered from his disorders after intense therapy. He eventually wrote his book as a way to share his experiences and help others cope.

Addictive Personalities

Another group at risk for exercise addiction comprises people who are born with addictive personalities. This means these people more easily lose control over a habit, such as smoking or exercising, to the point that the habit becomes the center of their lives. There is debate about whether or not a person is truly born with an addictive personality, but many psychologists contend that the addictive personality, whether innate or developed, is a distinct psychological trait that predisposes particular individuals to addictions.

Many experts believe addictive personalities result from a combination of biological, psychological, and environmental factors. Typically people with addictive personalities use their addictions to deal with stress, fear, anger, or grief. Often they also suffer from low self-esteem and experience anxiety and depression; as a result they become addicted to either substances or behaviors as a coping mechanism to suppress their anxiety and depression.

An addictive personality who starts jogging or running has a greater chance of letting running control his or her life. Chris Barber, a writer for fitness magazines, writes about how some long-distance runners show signs of addictive personalities.

Barber believes that a line exists that certain runners cross when their discipline and training turn into an addiction. "There are many signs of an addiction, but the universal result of an addiction is when it becomes an overbearing aspect of your life," he writes.

> This all consuming addiction leads you to neglect other portions of your life. Distance running has fallen into this category for some runners. They get up at 3 a.m. to go for a run, often missing social activities from the night before. Some distance runners may go to work exhausted after their morning run, hurting their productivity and career, much like an alcoholic who comes to work with a hangover.[34]

Switching Addictions

Often people with addictive personalities may beat one addiction only to end up replacing it with another. Rory Coleman is an example of a person who switched addictions. More than a decade ago, he was an overweight alcoholic who smoked forty cigarettes a day. When he was told by a doctor that he would unlikely live to age forty unless he changed his habits, Coleman stopped smoking and drinking and began to run. Since then he has run in more than six hundred marathons.

Coleman typically runs 100 miles (161km) a week. He claims he is not addicted and says, "I'm somebody that needs exercise. I don't ever intend to stop. But I'm not addicted to running. I've just made it a part of my life. And it's a positive thing—have you ever met a heroin addict who says they enjoy it?"[35] Many health professionals, however, would contend that Coleman is an exercise addict, based on his addictions in the past and his current stringent and overzealous attitude toward exercise. Coleman does admit that he has covered more than 25,000 miles (40,250km) while running in the past seven years.

Mimi Anderson, who is in her late forties, also says her friends often tell her that she has exchanged one addiction for another. For fifteen years she suffered from anorexia, and although she has overcome that addiction she is now an "ultra-runner" who

Which Sports Are More Likely to Lead to Addiction?

There are certain sports that result in eating disorders, including exercise addiction, more than others because of the sport's focus on being thin. Sports such as gymnastics, figure skating, dancing, and synchronized swimming have a higher percentage of athletes with eating disorders than do sports such as basketball, skiing, and volleyball. This is because in the former the thinner (or lighter) a person is the better they tend to perform. At times coaches contribute to these addictions by requiring their athletes to be a specific weight or body mass. Some athletes will not only train for their sport but also start dieting or excessively exercising in order to attain as thin a body as possible; however, this often results in exhaustion, body fatigue, and even more serious physical problems.

Sports such as gymnastics, in which a low body weight is ideal, tend to produce a high percentage of exercise addicts.

competes on a regular basis in marathons in excess of 100 miles (161km). As an anorexic, Anderson severely limited her calorie intake as part of her addiction to food limitation. As an exercise addict, she allows herself to eat normally, but constantly exercises. In 2009 she broke the record for a female running the John O'Groats to Land's End marathon, which runs 840 miles (1352km) and covers the entire length of the island of Great Britain, from the southwest to the northeast. Anderson covered the distance in twelve days and fifteen hours, averaging 65 miles (105km) a day. Unlike Coleman, Anderson agrees that her running is an addiction, but she believes it is a healthy one despite the fact that it affects her family life. "Normally I run seven days a week, but my husband has told me I can only do six," she says. "He gets really cross with me. I've just got back from one race and I'm about to do another. It is an addiction, but it's a healthy one."[36]

Health professionals disagree with Anderson about exercise addiction being a healthy one. Although intense exercise can be healthy, an exercise addict can easily cross the line from healthy to dangerous. When exercise addicts continue to exercise beyond pain, injury, or exhaustion, the addicts can experience serious damage. Additionally, exercise addicts often emotionally hurt themselves, friends, and family members by withdrawing from them in order to exercise. No matter what has led a person to exercise addiction, all exercise addicts put themselves in danger of harm.

CHAPTER FOUR

The Dangers of Exercise Addiction

Regular exercise is good for the body. Doctors, nurses, and other health care professionals recommend that people get regular cardiovascular exercise and strength training in order to keep their bodies as healthy as possible. Even the U.S. government recommends that people work out in order to maintain good health. According to the 2008 Physical Activity Guidelines for Americans, a person should do at least 150 minutes of moderate cardio activity, such as brisk walking, in a week and twice a week should engage in muscle-strengthening activities. A person can increase the number and intensity of these exercises in order to speed up the results.

However, as with most things in life, a person can get too much of a good thing, including exercise. According to the University of Pennsylvania's Office of Health Education, for an average person who is not an athlete or in training for an event, exercise beyond burning thirty-five hundred calories per week, which is equivalent to six hours of running a week or seven and a half hours of tennis, leads to decreased physical benefits and increased risk of injury. "My recommendation for the average person would be to work out three to five times per week for at least 30 minutes at a moderate intensity," Creighton University Medical Center doctor of physical therapy Matt Briggs says. "Even the most elite athletes would not be able to keep [three-hour daily workouts] of volume at a high intensity of working out every day for a prolonged period of time and stay healthy."[37]

The extreme regimens of exercise addicts can lead to insomnia, depression, and fatigue. Other physical side effects include muscular and skeletal injuries, such as shin splits, bone fractures, arthritis, or damage to cartilage and ligaments. Exercise addicts put themselves at risk for all of these damages.

An exercise addict can also adversely affect his or her emotional state and social life due to extreme exercise regimens. Emotionally, an exercise addict often experiences excessive guilt, to the point that they become depressed, when they miss a workout. Socially, they may alienate loved ones to the point that relationships are broken.

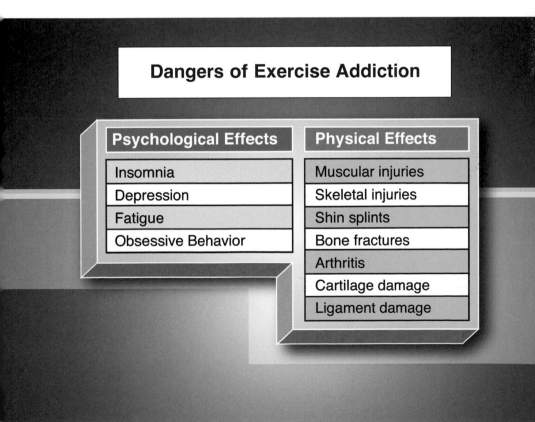

Dangers of Exercise Addiction

Psychological Effects	Physical Effects
Insomnia	Muscular injuries
Depression	Skeletal injuries
Fatigue	Shin splints
Obsessive Behavior	Bone fractures
	Arthritis
	Cartilage damage
	Ligament damage

Initial Symptoms

Initially exercise addicts will not see the negative aspects of their addiction. Instead they will see only the positive physical benefits of their exercise because they will likely gain muscle, lose fat, and see a gain in their cardio conditioning. After time, however, if their overexercising continues, exercise addicts will see a decline in their physical health.

The first symptoms of overexercising are insomnia and an elevated heart rate when waking in the morning. Also, an addict may experience exhaustion and a weakened immune system, which makes him or her more likely to catch colds and the flu. Addicts are more likely to get stress fractures and torn ligaments. Additionally, when running or biking, an addict's legs may feel heavier than in the past, and after running he or she will not recover as well as before.

Often exercise addicts will ignore their body's warning signs and continue their workouts, ultimately causing more problems. Michelle Biton, a health and nutrition coach, has seen the symptoms of exercise addiction in some of her clients. The most common symptom she observes is people exercising even when they are putting themselves at risk of getting hurt. "A previous client illustrated this obsession very well. A woman ran a marathon with acute shin splints and trained for a triathlon with her arm in a cast," Biton writes, "Despite doctors forbidding her from exercise for fear she could permanently damage her wrist, she continued to abuse her body because of her intense fear of weight gain."[38]

Long-Term Physical Problems

Serious physical problems can result from an exercise addict's continual extreme exercising. One result may be the increased production of cortisol, a hormone produced in response to stress, which can cause the breakdown of bone. This leads to a higher risk of stress fractures and osteoporosis, a disease of the bones where the bone mineral density is reduced. Additionally, exercise addiction can lead to muscle wasting, or the loss of muscle tissue, which can result in a person's being unable

A Starved Body Gets Hyperactive

A potential danger for an exercise addict is that his or her body may become hyperactive. Scientists have found that starved people who are not getting enough calories due to lack of eating and/or overexercising may have a surprising reaction—they may become hyperactive, which means they have the tendency to keep moving even though this expends yet more calories. As a result the person loses more weight and faces the physical dangers of starvation. This response has been observed in starving animals; for example, studies have found that most mammals become restless and agitated when experiencing hunger. Another study discovered that laboratory rats starved down to 70 percent of their body weight stop eating and become hyperactive, spinning up to 12 miles (19km) a day on their tiny exercise wheels. In humans, the result of hyperactivity combined with restricted calories and excessive exercise is an increase in the dangers a body experiences when starved and overexhausted from lack of calories and too much exertion.

A study found lab rats starved to 70 percent of their body weight stop eating and spin up to 12 miles a day on their exercise wheels.

to perform certain tasks, such as walking, or can worsen the risk of accidents while performing those tasks.

There are some specific dangers to both men and women. In men, excessive exercise can lead to decreased production of testosterone, a syndrome known as hypogonadism, which can lead to infertility, loss of muscle mass, and loss of bone mass. Among women, there is risk of amenorrhoea, the absence of the menstrual period, during which hormones, such as estrogen, shut down. This leads to loss of calcium in the bones, making them brittle and prone to breaking. It also can result in fertility problems in later years.

Broken bones are a problem for both men and women who overexercise and refuse to take enough time to heal when a fracture does occur. Alexa (not her real name) ended up suffering from long-term problems due to her overexercising and the fact that she would not allow her body to heal.

Alexa used to begin her days with an 8-mile (12.8km) run, walked at lunch time, then ended her days at the gym. She was in her twenties and lean and muscular, looking healthy and fit; however, she was hurting both emotionally and physically. Alexa was unhappy with her life—she hated her job, did not see her friends much, and put exercise at the center of her life. As a result, she began to experience physical problems. "The breaking point came in 1998 when Alexa hit the road the day after running her first marathon," writes Robin Rinaldi of *Runner's World*. "She tried to ignore the searing pain in her pelvis, but could not. Years of overexercise had depleted her body of estrogen, irreversibly damaging her bones and leaving her with multiple stress fractures in her pelvis."[39] After this point, Alexa gradually stopped abusing exercise in order to help her physical and emotional states. Now thirty years old, she runs about 35 miles (56km) per week, but keeps her routine to once a day, six days a week.

Serious Issues

The most serious outcome that can occur from extreme exercise is of course death. Exercise addiction can result in a person's experiencing heart arrhythmias, which occur when the electrical impulses in the heart that coordinate heartbeats do not function properly and cause the heart to beat too fast, too slowly, or irregularly. Arrhythmias can lead to serious problems, including strokes and heart attacks. Ventricular fibrillation is one type of arrhythmia that is deadly. It occurs when the heart beats with rapid, erratic electrical impulses that cause the pumping chambers in the heart to simply quiver uselessly, instead of pumping blood. Then a person's blood pressure plummets, which cuts off blood supply to the vital organs. A person with ventricular fibrillation will collapse within seconds and soon will not be breathing or have a pulse.

Charlotte thought she was going to die due to problems resulting from her excessive exercising. She used to work out twice a day for a total of six hours. During one workout she ran a marathon distance of 26.2 miles (42km) and then went to the gym for a kickboxing class because she feared missing even one session. Her workouts caught up with her body and one day she fainted after a kickboxing class and experienced a heart arrhythmia—she remembers feeling like she would die.

Luckily, Charlotte recovered from that episode but soon found that her exercise addiction caused potentially lifelong physical problems. She was diagnosed with hypothyroidism, a condition in which the thyroid gland does not produce enough of certain important hormones, due to her thyroid being suppressed as a result of overexercising. Untreated hypothyroidism can cause a number of health problems, such as obesity, joint pain, infertility, and heart disease; however, it is easily treated with an oral medicine that restores normal hormone levels. Since she was diagnosed, Charlotte has begun to develop a better emotional relationship with exercise, but she still struggles. "It's improving but it's probably a battle I'll fight for the rest of my life,"[40] she admits.

Kristin Seifried also endangered her life with excessive exercise. Seifried was at the gym every day after dinner for at least two hours. She typically did an hour of weight lifting followed by another one to two hours on the elliptical trainer. One night, soon

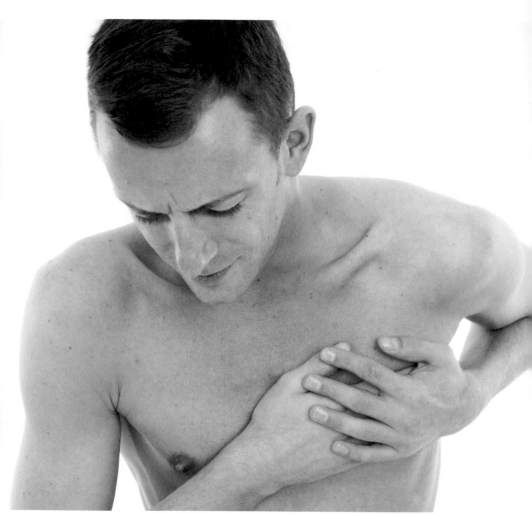

Extreme exercising can lead to arrhythmia, a condition in which the heart beats with erratic electrical impulses that cause the heart to quiver instead of pumping blood.

after the birth of her second child, she arrived at the gym and felt exhausted. She would not give herself a break though and, after someone complimented her on how lean she looked, decided she might even do an extra workout. She continued with this type of routine and mindset until a major health problem occurred. After three years, Seifried was hospitalized for pericarditis, a potentially fatal viral infection that attacks the pericardium, the sac surrounding the heart. Because of all her gym time, Seifried's body fat percentage was so low that her immune system was not able to handle the virus, landing her in intensive care. Seifried was lucky to recover and at that point decided she needed treatment to help overcome her addiction.

Excessive Guilt

Another common problem with exercise addiction is that exercise becomes the center of the addicts' lives and results in their feeling extremely guilt if they cannot exercise. Exercise

Excessive workouts can lead to pericarditis, a viral infection that calcifies the pericardial sac (white) surrounding the heart, which can be fatal.

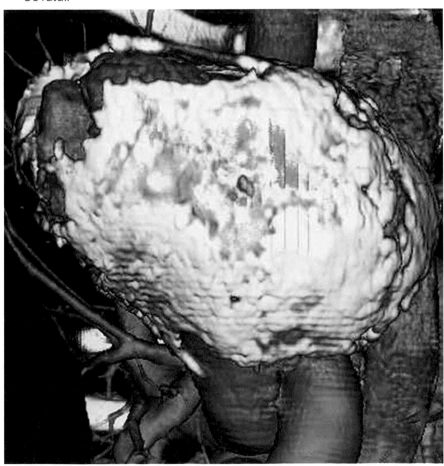

becomes an obsession that they must fulfill in order not to feel out of control or depressed. Exercise addicts can suffer withdrawal symptoms, including sleep problems, depression, anxiety, confusion, and difficulty concentrating when they miss a day of working out. What may have started as an enjoyable and healthy hobby, such as running, leads to an unhappy existence.

Melanie Jenkins (not her real name) got to the point that she experienced excessive guilt if she even considered missing a workout. The twenty-seven-year-old graduate student was an avid marathon runner, cyclist, and fitness instructor. While training to improve her marathon time, she increased her running to six days a week and instead of limiting herself to one long run, between 12 and 18 miles (19–29km) a week, as experts recommend, she ran two to six long-distance runs. During this training, she also continued swimming and cycling regularly and taught fitness classes. Soon she developed knee problems, was also having trouble sleeping, and had become uncharacteristically moody.

Jenkins knew she should take time off from her fitness routine, but emotionally she could not. "A part of me was afraid to stop," she says. "I was afraid to take days off. I worried excessively about losing my fitness and gaining weight. Resting seemed like a waste of time. It was something I knew I should do, but never could seem to get around to."[41] Instead of taking time off, Jenkins continued working out, and her body and mind suffered. Finally, she realized the toll overexercising was placing on her body and was able to reduce her workouts.

Some exercise addicts find they cannot function if they do not get their daily exercise. At age nineteen, Jen Sacket trains with her college volleyball team in a program designed to increase her vertical jump and endurance through plymetrics, a type of exercise training whereby the person repeats certain movements in which a muscle is loaded and then contracted in rapid sequence. She also engages in strength training. In addition to that, she runs long distances to keep in what she considers good shape. However, Sacket has started to feel the emotional effects that are considered symptoms of an exercise addiction. She notices her stress level increasing if she misses too many days of exercise. "I start to feel like I have less energy and motivation to get my work done," she says. "I start to feel overwhelmed with school."[42] Exercise addicts often find that they feel out of control and panicky if they miss their exercise routines, which makes their entire lives more stressful.

Social Impacts

Exercise addicts also harm their social lives because they make exercise their number one priority. They will miss out on social events or gatherings if these events conflict with their workouts. Their workouts come first, ultimately upsetting their relationships with friends and family.

Melissa Henriquez knows what it is like to deal with compulsive exercising's impacts on relationships. Henriquez first became addicted to working out six months after starting Weight Watchers. She was twenty-five and was excited about her weight loss and the positive changes in her body. Henriquez added exercise to her routine to lose more weight and achieve a fitter body. She started to go to the gym in her apartment building at 5:30 every morning and do a minimum of an hour of cardio. Three days a week she would also do weight lifting following the cardio. She soon added more workouts to what had been a healthy routine, making it an unhealthy obsession. In addition to her morning workouts, she would go to spinning and Body Pump (a muscle-toning and fitness routine) classes on Saturdays and most nights would go back to the gym for more cardio.

It got to the point where Henriquez was exercising twice a day and would not miss a day without feeling extremely guilty. She went almost an entire year missing social events to ensure she got her daily workouts. At the time her boyfriend lived in another country so she was able to get these workouts in without adversely affecting their relationship, but this soon changed when she and her boyfriend married.

Once married, Henriquez and her husband lived together, and he saw how stringent her daily exercise routine was. He became concerned about how much time she spent exercising and worrying about exercising. Henriquez herself realized her

Severe Dehydration

One physical danger associated with exercise addiction is severe dehydration, in which the body is depleted of needed fluids. This condition results when exercise addicts lose fluids through perspiring during heavy workouts. Additionally, exercise addicts disregard the weather and even work out on severely hot and sunny days, raising their risk of dehydration. According to the Mayo Clinic, "The longer you exercise, the more difficult it is to stay hydrated. During exercise, your body can absorb about 24 to 32 ounces (.7L to .9L) of water an hour, but you may lose twice that amount in hot weather." Severe dehydration can be quite serious, with symptoms that include dizziness, elevated heart rate, fever, and even unconsciousness or delirium. Untreated, dehydration can lead to swelling of the brain, seizures, and kidney failure. People who are severely dehydrated need to get emergency room treatment where they will get the necessary salts and fluids intravenously rather than by mouth.

Mayo Clinic, "Dehydration," July 25, 2009. www.mayoclinic.com/health/dehydration/DS00561/D SECTION=risk-factors.

During exercise the body can absorb about 24 to 32 ounces of water an hour, but can lose twice that amount in hot weather.

exercise had become a problem when her husband surprised her with a romantic trip. Instead of being elated, she was stressed because of the idea of missing her workouts. "My husband wanted to take me to Chicago for the day as a surprise, an impromptu 'let's go and have fun in the city'. . . and I freaked because I had it in my head I would work out and here he was throwing me for a total loop," she writes. "I still remember the pained, dejected look on his face and it was in that moment that I realized my sick obsession with exercise was interfering with my marriage and my life."[43]

Loss of Joy

Exercise addiction also results in a person no longer enjoying much else about his or her life besides exercising. To addicts, even exercise eventually becomes something that *has* to be done instead of something fun or joyful. Exercise addicts may experience depression, even as they exercise, which worsens, initially, if they stop exercising.

Larry Brown let running take over his life to the point it was no longer about fun, but about something he had to do. He was in his early forties and running 50 miles (80km) a week, and he let running consume his thoughts. If he could not run due to reasons beyond his control, he became angry and upset. Even when he was diagnosed with prostate cancer and developed a tumor in his leg, his first thought was running. "That was my first question," says Brown. "Not whether I could still work, or whether I'd be able to walk. It was 'Can I keep running?'"[44]

Eventually, Brown realized that his running had become more important than other aspects of his life, including his own health. He focused on fighting the cancer and had his last treatment in 1995. He continues to run but on a less intense basis, logging 20 miles (32km) a week with a day off on Mondays. As a result, he enjoys and controls his exercise now, rather than letting it control him. "I feel like there is more joy and less intensity,"[45] he says.

The Lowest Point

Exercise addiction can spiral to the point where addicts feel totally out of control and with no hope of getting better. They may see themselves getting sicker and injuring themselves from their exercise, but they cannot stop, and they feel there is no way out of the cycle. This happened to Jamie-Lynn DiScala, who played Meadow on *The Sopranos*. She suffered from exercise addiction for years, beginning when she was a teenager.

DiScala said her battle with the disorder began after her high school boyfriend broke up with her. She became depressed and focused on her looks and body, becoming obsessed about burning calories by exercising. She started doing twenty minutes on the treadmill before school, which soon turned into waking up at 3:00 A.M. in order to work out for four hours before school. Within four months her weight had dropped to a dangerous 80 pounds (36kg).

She would look at her reflection and see her bones and ribs sticking out, but could not stop herself. Her life revolved around calorie counting, exercise, and weight. She was so depressed that

Actress Jamie-Lynn DiScala relates her recovery from exercise addiction in her autobiography *Wise Girl*.

she thought there was no way to get better. "I seriously contemplated suicide," said DiScala. "I felt that no one in this world would ever understand the constant battle I had in my head every day."[46] Luckily, DiScala's parents recognized that she had a problem and turned to a nutritionist and a psychiatrist for help. With their help, DiScala was able to overcome her disorders and share her experiences in her autobiography *Wise Girl.*

It was a long road for DiScala to recover from her issues with eating and exercise. Through much emotional work she has developed healthy habits that allow her body and mind to recover, exemplifying the successful treatment options available to recovering exercise addicts.

CHAPTER FIVE

How Is Exercise Addiction Treated?

Like any addiction, before exercise addiction can be success-fully treated the addict must recognize and admit that he or she is an addict. Often the addict will reach a crisis that makes him or her realize there is a problem. This crisis may be a health, social, career, or emotional crisis that wakes the addict up to the problem.

Noell Blevins was addicted to exercise but would not admit it, even though it was affecting her emotionally and physically. Exercise was the main focus of her day to the point that if she did not complete her self-imposed exercise regimen she be-came moody and upset. "Before teaching a class I would do a 5 mile (8km) 'warm up' on the treadmill or five mile 'cool down' afterwards. Crazy. But to me, then, it was normal,"[47] she writes. She continued like this until the summer of 2009, when her body rebelled.

It took severe physical pain for Blevins to realize she was addicted to exercise.

I vividly remember sitting on the back deck of the . . . house last summer, around the fourth of July. I was de-pressed. I was in excruciating pain. I was in withdrawal. My hips were causing me unimaginable pain and there was no end in sight. . . . I felt hopeless and overwhelmed. My friend Beth was up visiting and I remember nearly crying trying to figure out how I was going to exercise and make it to September [when her doctor could see her]. She looked at me like I was insane. Exercise??? Seriously? Is that what you're worried about?[48]

Sometimes it takes a painful injury for exercise addicts to realize they are addicted to exercise.

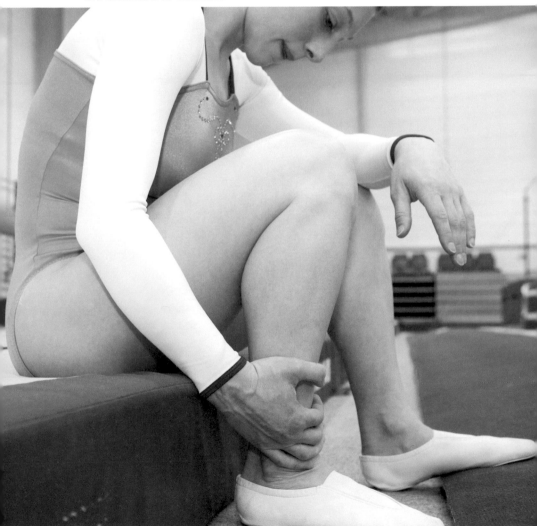

PIRT Method of Counseling

Ira M. Sacker, M.D., founder, president, and medical director of the nonprofit HEED Foundation (Helping End Eating Disorders), has written a book titled *Regaining Your Self: A Bold New Approach to Overcoming Eating Disorders.* In it he recommends personal interactive rational therapy (PIRT) as a way to help people overcome psychological disorders such as exercise addiction. PIRT is an approach that combines personal, interactive, and rational sessions of therapy. During the sessions patients and a doctor share life stories and talk about themselves. The rational aspect involves helping patients clearly see themselves by discussing with them how it is that their anxieties and obsession with being perfect causes their destructive habits. "In our sessions I'm not distant from my patients and I don't see them as just cases—they're real people, and I've found that they respond best when I reveal aspects of my personality to them," says Sacker. "Our sessions are interactive. The rational aspect of therapy is crucial. Eating disorder patients generally can't see themselves clearly—they need a therapist's help to see the reality of their condition and to grasp the ways out of it." Sacker will talk about personal aspects of his life, such as that he is an overachiever and perfectionist and he can empathize with his patients' obsessions. Sacker believes that patients get better when they develop a strong personal relationship with the therapist in addition to having someone help them see things more clearly.

Ira Sacker, "Discovering the Self," 2007. www.hyperionbooks.com/titleexcerpt.asp?ISBN=1401303056.

PIRT (personal interactive rational therapy) requires personal and interactive sessions with a doctor.

Both the pain and her friend's reaction made Blevins realize how addicted to exercise she had become. This crisis woke her up to the emotional and physical problems excessive exercise was causing her, and she began to go down the road to recovery. Today she works out on a normal schedule consisting of about four hours of swimming and two Pilates classes a week.

Diagnosis

Sometimes friends or family can help addicts recognize their addictions by confronting them about it. This may allow the addicts to see their exercise habits from another viewpoint and admit they are addicted. Friends or loved ones who suspect someone is suffering from exercise addiction can look for certain signs to confirm their suspicions.

Peach Friedman, now a spokeswoman for the National Eating Disorders Association and a personal trainer, suffered from both exercise addiction and eating disorders. After much counseling she conquered these disorders and wrote a book, *Diary of an Exercise Addict*, about her battle. She tells people that there are five major symptoms that an exercise addict typically exhibits:

> First is a devotion to a regimented form of exercise—the same machine, the same gym, same time every day, no flexibility. Second is excessively exercising and intense fear of states of relaxation, like "I will not drive to the store, I will walk to the store to burn 100 extra calories." Third is prioritization of gym over all other activities (including family birthdays, dating and work). Fourth is equating your identity with exercise, like "I do not know who I would be without it." Fifth is motivation by guilt, fear, anxiety or punishment, like "I'm exercising today because I feel I have not earned my dinner," or "eating cake equals more running." Healthy motivations include wanting to clear your head, jog with friends or take care of your health.[49]

Additionally, people can use criteria developed by Heather A. Hausenblas of the University of Florida and Danielle

Symons Downs of Pennsylvania State University to determine whether they are dependent on exercise. The criteria are based on those in the American Psychiatric Association's *Diagnostic and Statistical Manual for Mental Disorders* for determining substance dependency and on Hausenblas and Downs's research in the exercise field.

Hausenblas and Downs developed seven criteria for people to use to determine whether they are exercise addicts; if they meet three of the criteria, they are considered dependent on exercise. The criteria include (1) whether a person has developed tolerance, a need for increased amounts of exercise to achieve desired effect and diminished effect with continued use of same amount of exercise; (2) withdrawal, which includes symptoms such as anxiety or fatigue when exercise is stopped; (3) intention effect: when exercise is often taken in larger amounts or over a longer period than was intended; (4) lack of control, a persistent desire or unsuccessful effort to cut down or control exercise; (5) time: a great deal of time is spent participating in activities necessary to obtain exercise; (6) reduction in other activities: social, occupational, or recreational activities are given up or reduced because of exercise; and (7) continuance, when exercise is continued despite knowing that a persistent and/or recurring physical or psychological problem is likely to have been caused or exacerbated by the exercising.

Overview of Health

The good news is that exercise addiction, like any other addiction, can be treated in a variety of ways. Before treatment, an addict's overall health and personality should be reviewed by a health professional. This will help determine the best type of treatment for the addict.

First, a doctor should review the physical health of the addict to see whether any special medical treatment, such as addressing sprains, exhaustion, dehydration, or other issues, is needed. Additionally, according to Edward Cumella, director of research and education at Remuda Ranch Programs for Eating Disorders, an exercise addict should undergo at least one assessment with a dietitian to ensure the addict understands

As part of treatment, exercise addicts should consult with a dietician to ensure they are getting all their nutritional requirements.

what nutrition he or she truly needs. Also, the doctor and nutritionist can help determine whether the addict is getting enough nutrition and is medically stable to continue engaging in moderate exercise or sports during treatment.

What also should be assessed is whether the exercise addict also has an eating disorder. "Patients with significant eating disorder behaviors are at a high risk of EA [exercise addiction] relapse and medical complications from the combined eating disorder and EA," writes Cumella. "Eating disorder behaviors therefore must be reduced before exercise resumption, including normalizing eating, stabilizing weight, and decreasing bingeing/purging."[50] No matter what treatment is called for, Cumella believes that a person with an eating

Breathing to Recovery

Remuda Ranch, a treatment center that focuses on eating disorders and exercise addiction, uses FORM movement as a way to help people with eating and exercise disorders. FORM stands for Freedom Ordered Renewal Meditative Movement and was developed by Kathryn Linehan, a documentary filmmaker and fitness teacher from Los Angeles. It is is a meditative movement technique, similar to Pilates, that is accompanied by deep breathing, stretching, specialized music, and readings from the Bible and is performed twice a week by patients at Remuda Ranch. "FORM teaches patients to breath deeply and stretch, easing the body aches and pains they may have because of their eating disorder," said Amy Gerberry, director of activities at Remuda Programs for Eating Disorders. "FORM also teaches compulsive exercisers to be more moderate in their exercise routines and helps improve trust and body image through the experience of acceptance by other participants in the class and techniques that teach people to welcome God's help in life's struggles."

Remuda Ranch, "New Movement Therapy Helps Those with Eating Disorders," 2010. www.remudaranch.com/Resources/news_detail.aspx?article=5734407.

FORM (Freedom Ordered Renewal Meditative Movement) is a meditative technique involving breathing and stretching exercises.

disorder and exercise addiction needs to cease any exercise activity until the eating disorder has been overcome.

Emotional State

In addition to their physical states, exercise addicts' emotional states must be assessed to help understand how best to treat them. According to Cumella, patients' motivation to conquer their exercise addiction must be evaluated. If addicts have a very strong motivation to break their habits, then it is likely they do not need constant oversight during treatment. Others, however, who are getting treatment merely because of external factors such as being forced by parents, doctors, or school, must be monitored more carefully because they may mask their true problem in order to just "get through" treatment to satisfy others. They may sneak in excessive exercise unless they are monitored.

An addict's body image is also of concern when determining treatment. An addict whose exercise is tied to body image will need counseling specific to body-image issues and self-worth. Addicts with a poor view of their bodies will need counseling or other therapy to help them develop self-esteem based on attributes apart from appearance.

To Exercise or Not to Exercise

One issue that is often debated is whether or not an exercise addict should be allowed to exercise during treatment. With most addictions, a complete stoppage of the habit, such as from using drugs or alcohol, is required in order for an addict to recover. This is because the addiction is a negative one, and not even a small amount of drugs or alcohol is good for the person. Exercise, on the other hand, is good for people, even exercise addicts, provided the recommended amount of exercise is not exceeded. What is debated is whether the exercise addict can emotionally handle even a small amount of exercise during his or her treatment.

Some believe the addict must cease all exercise during treatment in order to get a handle on the addiction and conquer it. Debbie Mandel, author of *Turn on Your Inner Light*, has studied fitness and exercise for years and believes exercise addicts need to take time off completely from exercise in order to heal emotionally. Mandel says:

> To break an exercise addiction, which is evidenced by more than 90 minutes of continuous exercise 7 days a week, the prescription calls for no vigorous exercise for one month. Overtraining causes feelings of worthlessness and depression. By resting the body, we heal the mind. We face our inner demons that drive us to overload our muscles and connective tissues. The hardest thing to accept is living in ambiguity.[51]

Mandel believes that both the body and mind will heal during this period, allowing the person to come back to exercising with a new attitude.

Others believe that gradually reducing an addict's schedule is a better approach than stopping the exercise all at once. Sandra Levy Ceren is a clinical psychologist with more than forty years of experience who believes the best approach is to wean exercise addicts off their schedule one exercise at a time. "Exercise addicts are single-minded. . . . This is what defines them, what they are going to do and they don't want to hear anything about it," says Ceren. "So I'll start by asking them to do a little less and see if they felt any worse for it."[52]

Cumella also believes that an exercise addict can exercise during treatment provided he or she is physically in good health and not battling an eating disorder. She says,

> Once patients are medically stable, education and practice in healthy exercise should begin, perhaps involving an exercise physiologist, athletic trainer, physical therapist, or dietitian skilled in this area. In making recommendations for healthy exercise—including return to professional sports—providers should work to minimize relapse risk and current/future health problems. Recommendations for exercise should be discussed with and agreed upon by patients. A written terms of participation contract [a written agreement between the patients and those treating them specifying the rules of treatment] between patients

and the treatment team and, when appropriate, athletic departments and family, is useful.[53]

Ultimately, whether or not an addict exercises during the recovery is up to the addict and the overseer of the treatment.

Blogging to Health

There are several different types of treatment a person can try to overcome an exercise addiction. Some addicts choose to beat their addictions on their own and find various ways to break their obsessions and change their behaviors. When addicts deal with the obsession on their own, they still need to find the reason behind their obsession in order to come to grips with what is making them exercise excessively. Many experts recommend that addicts journal about their feelings in order to get a handle on what is causing them to overexercise. Debbie Mandel believes that both meditating and journaling is key to getting to an exercise addict's root problems. She says,

> The addict needs to meditate even if just for five minutes a day using a personal affirmation for serenity as a springboard to developing her emotional/spiritual side. Alternatively doing some sort of moving meditation, like going on a nature walk, will help align body and mind. Journaling during the day helps expose the root of unhappiness. Many deep thoughts emerge while one is writing. The goal of meditation and journaling is to increase focused attention. Instead of generating wild, distracted energy, the exerciser would concentrate her energy.[54]

An open form of journaling helped Melissa Henriquez overcome her exercise addiction. Henriquez attended some cognitive therapy sessions but really felt her blog, an online journal of her battle, helped her more than the therapy did to understand herself and her addiction. Henriquez says,

> I began blogging as a way to unearth my dirty secret in the hopes of raising awareness of this taboo problem (eating and exercise disorders) affecting nearly 60 percent of women. It's something people just don't talk about, and I figured if I could serve as an advocate and help just one

person . . . I'd know I was doing the right thing. And so far, I feel like I've absolutely made the right decision to blog. While my blog itself will likely evolve . . . I know it's been a cathartic outlet for me and I wouldn't change the experience I've had for a second.[55]

Since beginning her blog Henriquez has become a healthy eater and exerciser.

At eating disorder treatment centers, like this one in North Carolina, patients talk to doctors about what exercise means to them as part of the therapy.

Counseling

For Peach Friedman, counseling was the best way to overcome her exercise addiction. In 2000, after a breakup with her boyfriend and her parents' separation, Friedman felt out of control. She began to use exercise as a way to regain control in her life. She started out with a healthy routine—thirty minutes on the treadmill and the occasional yoga class—but this soon spiraled into an exercise addiction.

Friedman went from a fit 145 pounds (66kg) at 5 feet 9 inches (175cm) to a skeletal 100 pounds (45kg) in only three months. She started every day with a 10-mile (16km) run and ended it with dance classes or swimming or more running and also limiting herself to as few as eight hundred calories a day. Friedman could not make it through a day without exercise, to the point that she once exercised five hundred days in a row. Friends and family noticed her problem, and with their support, Friedman realized she needed help.

Friedman, in college at the time, decided not to return to school and moved back home to attend both individual and group therapy in addition to weekly meetings with a local dietitian. After three years of treatment, she felt healthy enough to move out and work toward her master's degree. Today she weighs a healthy 165 pounds (75kg) and works as a personal trainer. She shares her experiences in her book, *Diary of an Exercise Addict*. Friedman has stated that it took years of therapy to get her to recovery and where she is today, and she still attends therapy to keep herself on track.

Treatment Centers

Some exercise addicts find that attending a treatment center is the best option for them because it takes them away from their everyday lives and allows them to focus solely on recovery. While living at the treatment center, they attend both group and individual counseling sessions to help gain a better understanding of their emotions and what underlies their exercise addiction. Additionally, they meet with nutritionists to learn what is healthy for their bodies and how to change their eating habits.

One of the most important issues addicts address at a treatment center is what is driving them to exercise. Carolyn Ross, a physician at the Eating Disorder Center of Denver, says, "The biggest thing I've learned [about exercise addicts] is to find out what the exercise represents to them," Ross says. "For some it's distraction from fears and anxieties, for others it can be an escape. They will tell you that their exercise is saving them. Doctors have to know what it's saving them from."[56] Once doctors understand that, they work with their patients to find better ways to deal with the fears and anxieties.

Lindsay Adcock began excessively working out to deal with loneliness and abandonment issues. She tried several times to recover from exercise addiction and bulimia without attending a treatment center but each time would fall back on her compulsive behavior. Eventually, she was hospitalized for liver problems and hip arthritis, and following the hospital stay, she chose to enter the Eating Disorder Center of Denver's hospitalization program. For months she attended nutrition, addiction, and behavioral classes for fourteen hours a day. She was monitored during the other ten hours, including when she slept. This constant oversight and counseling, plus antidepressants, helped her control her anxieties and deal with the loneliness that was her underlying problem. Adcock was eventually able to return to moderate amounts of exercise and a healthy life after having found other ways to deal with her anxieties and loneliness. "I have my exercise back and it's fun now," says Adcock, who now works out with friends through kickboxing and lifting weights. "I used to work out because I felt like I had to. Now I actually enjoy doing it."[57]

Adcock feels she was fortunate to get into treatment before her addiction took an even greater toll on her mind and body. Recovery is considered possible if an addict finds the right treatment method for him or her and is ready to make a true change. Although there are no specific statistics for the recovery of exercise addicts, there are statistics for related disorders that indicate success is possible. According to the University of Maryland Medical Center, anorexia recovery rates vary between 23 and 50 percent. The Eating Disorders

Venture reports that bulimia patients have a 50 percent chance of recovery after five to ten years. Exercise addicts, whose treatment is similar to that of bulimics, have a similar prognosis for recovery and a chance to regain their emotional and physical health.

Notes

Introduction: Out of Control

1. Paul Egan, "Exercise, Too Little of a Good Thing," The Cleveland Clinic. http://my.clevelandclinic.org/heart/prevention/exercise/exart_egan.aspx.
2. Quoted in Tamekia Reece, "Exercise Excess: You Can Have Too Much of a Good Thing," *Current Health 2*, October 2007. www.britannica.com/bps/additionalcontent/18/31683138/Exercise-Excess.
3. Quoted in Reece, "Exercise Excess."
4. Quoted in Reece, "Exercise Excess."
5. Quoted in Reece, "Exercise Excess."

Chapter One: What Is Exercise Addiction?

6. Jessica Girdwain, "Confessions of a Cardioholic," *Fitness*, March 2010, p. 117.
7. U.S. Department of Health and Human Services, "Physical Activity Has Many Health Benefits," October 16, 2008. www.health.gov/paguidelines/guidelines/chapter2.aspx.
8. Elizabeth Krieger, Caremark, "Addicted to Exercise," July 31, 2009. www.caremark.com/wps/portal/HEALTH_RESOURCES?topic=exerciseessay.
9. Elizabeth Quinn, "Compulsive Exercise in Athletes," About.com, February 13, 2008. http://sportsmedicine.about.com/cs/eatingdisorders1/a/compulsive_ex.htm.
10. Pauline Powers and Ron Thompson, *Exercise Balance*. Carlsbad, CA: Gurze Books, 2008. p. 46.
11. Men Get Eating Disorders Too! "Nigel's Story." www.mengetedstoo.co.uk/index.php/personal-stories/96-nigels-story-compulsive-exercise-and-anorexia.html.
12. K. Cossaboon, Hub Pages, "Exercise and the 'Endorphin Rush,'" 2010. http://hubpages.com/hub/ExerciseandTheEndorphinRush.

13. Quoted in Ed Harris, "Exercise Fanatics Suffer Withdrawal Like Drug Addicts Do," *London Evening Standard*, August 18, 2009. www.thisislondon.co.uk/standard/article-237336 93-exercise-fanatics-suffer-withdrawal-like-drug-addict.s.do.

14. Quoted in Tim Sprinkle, "Gotta Have It," *Trail Runner*, May 2006. www.trailrunnermag.com/article.php?id=91&cat=6.

15. Quoted in Sprinkle, "Gotta Have It."

Chapter Two: Exercise Addiction Is Tied to Other Disorders

16. Quoted in Krista Ramsey, "Starving to Have No Size at All," Cincinnati.com, March 8, 2010. http://news.cincinnati.com/article/20100308/NEWS01/3070383/Starving-to-have-no-size-at-all.

17. Quoted in Ramsey, "Starving to Have No Size at All."

18. Lindsey Hall and Leigh Cohn, "What Is Bulimia?" Bulimia .com. www.bulimia.com/client/client_pages/bulimia.cfm.

19. Jessica Setnick, "An RD Confesses: 'I had Bulimia,'" *Fitness*, March 2006. www.fitnessmagazine.com/health/body-image/stories/an-rd-confesses-i-had-bulimia/;jsessionid=JDG OVZAGLXNNQCQCEARCCZQ?page=1.

20. Brain Physics, "A Disorder or Just a Symptom?" 2010. www.brainphysics.com/exercise-addiction.php.

21. Quoted in A&E TV, "Cindee and Graham," www.aetv.com/obsessed/episode-guide.

22. Quoted in Chris Iliades, "The Distortion of Body Dysmorphic Disorder," Everyday Health, 2010. www.everydayhealth .com/eating-disorders/distorted-perspective-of-body-dysmorph ic-disorder.aspx.

23. Quoted in Michael Schwab, "We're All Men Here," Sex etc., April 18, 2008. www.sexetc.org/story/body_image/4642.

Chapter Three: Who Is Most at Risk for Exercise Addiction?

24. American Running Association, "Know the Signs of Unhealthy Exercise Addiction." www.active.com/running/Arti cles/Know_the_signs_of_unhealthy_exercise_addiction.htm.

25. Quoted in Lauren Cox, "Exercise Addicts Can Blame Their Brains," ABC News, August 28, 2009. http://abcnews.go .com/Health/MensHealthNews/story?id=8430744.

26. Michele Wallace, "Multi-Tri Training with Michele— Ironman and Exercise Addiction," San Diego Newsroom, September 2, 2009. http://sandiegonewsroom.com/news/in dex.php?option=com_content&view=article&id=35175:mul ti-tri-training-with-michele-ironman-and-exercise-addiction &catid=105:triathlons&Itemid=173.

27. Quoted in Sheba Wheeler, "Secret Sickness," *Denver Post*, May 5, 2008. .

28. Quoted in Karen Nelson, "Moderation: The Key to a Healthy Life?" *Tucson Citizen*, September 22, 2009. http://tucson citizen.com/kare/2009/09/22/moderation-the-secret-to-a- happy-life.

29. Quoted in Girdwain, "Confessions of a Cardioholic," p. 118.

30. Quoted in MedicineNet, "Exercise Excess," November 27, 2000. www.medicinenet.com/script/main/art.asp?article key=50963.

31. Quoted in Colin Fernandez, "How Lads' Mags Are Creating a Generation of Exercise-Obsessed Men Striving for the Perfect Body," *Daily Mail* (London), March 26, 2008. www.dailymail.co.uk/health/article-535690/How-lads-mags- creating-generation-exercise-obsessed-men-striving-perfect- body.html.

32. Quoted in CBS5, "Bigorexia: A Muscle Building Obsession," November 6, 2007. http://cbs5.com/health/bigorexia.muscle .building.2.570065.html.

33. Quoted in CBS, "The Skinny on Manorexia," September 30, 2008. www.cbsnews.com/stories/2008/09/30/earlyshow/ health/main4488410.shtml.

34. Chris Barber, "Running and Your Addictive Personality," Serious Running, June 17, 2009. www.seriousrunning .com/blog/health/running-and-your-addictive-personality.

35. Quoted in Tarquin Cooper, "Confessions of a Running Ad- dict," *Daily Telegraph* (London), August 24, 2009. www .telegraph.co.uk/health/dietandfitness/6066279/Confessions- of-a-running-addict.html.

36. Quoted in Cooper, "Confessions of a Running Addict."

Chapter Four: What Are the Dangers of Exercise Addiction?

37. Quoted in Melissa Kucirek, "Is Excessive Exercise Bad?" Suite 101, December 4, 2008. http://fitness.suite101.com/article.cfm/exercise_excessobsession_for_some#ixzz0trDJvJxo.
38. Michelle Biton, "Are You Exercise Obsessed?" Alive.com, September 2003. www.alive.com/1482a4a2.php?subject_bread_cramb=6.
39. Robin Rinaldi, "Running Nonstop," *Runners World*, August 2004. www.runnersworld.com/article/0,7120,s6-241-285--7174-0,00.html.
40. Quoted in Girdwain, "Confessions of a Cardioholic," p. 122.
41. Quoted in Stephanie Kinnon, "Avoid Overtraining," Active.com, 2010. www.active.com/women/Articles/avoid_overtraining.htm.
42. Quoted in Kucirek, "Is Excessive Exercise Bad?"
43. Melissa Henriquez, e-mail interview with author, June 24, 2010.
44. Quoted in Leslie Garcia, "When Exercise Takes Over," *Detroit Free Press*, May 30, 2010, p. 3D.
45. Quoted in Garcia, "When Exercise Takes Over," p. 3D.
46. Quoted in Melissa Lipman, "*Sopranos* star's struggle with eating disorder," CNN, November 7, 2005. www.cnn.com/2005/HEALTH/conditions/11/02/discala.eating.disorder/index.html.

Chapter Five: How Is Exercise Addiction Treated?

47. Noell Blevins, "Exercise Addiction?" April 1, 2010. http://noelblevins.blogspot.com/2010/04/exercise-addiction.html.
48. Blevins, "Exercise Addiction?"
49. Quoted in Carolyne Zinko, "Too Much Exercise Became an Addiction," *San Francisco Chronicle*, December 28, 2008. http://articles.sfgate.com/2008-12-28/living/17131676_1_exercise-addiction-exercise-bulimia-compulsive-exercise.

50. Edward Cumella, "The Heavy Weight of Exercise Addiction," *Behavioral Health Management*, September 1, 2005. www.allbusiness.com/health-care-social-assistance/850987-1.html.

51. Debbie Mandel, "Exercise Obsession," SheKnows, December 2008. www.sheknows.com/articles/2747/overcoming-exercise-addiction.

52. Quoted in Cassie Piercey, "Hooked on a Good Thing: When Exercise Becomes Addictive," San Diego News Network, May 11, 2010. www.sdnn.com/sandiego/2010-05-11/health-fitness/hooked-on-a-good-thing-when-exercise-becomes-ad dictive#ixzz0u9n5fKWG.

53. Cumella, "The Heavy Weight of Exercise Addiction."

54. Debbie Mandel, "Healing Exercise Addiction," *New Living Magazine*, February 2004. www.newliving.com/issues/feb_ 2004/articles/exercise%20addiction.html.

55. Melissa Henriquez, e-mail interview with author, June 24, 2010.

56. Quoted in Wheeler, "Secret Sickness."

57. Quoted in Wheeler, "Secret Sickness."

Glossary

addiction: The state of being controlled by a habit either psychologically or physically to such an extent that its cessation causes severe trauma.

anorexia: An eating disorder in which the person severely limits his or her calories to the point of near starvation.

body dysmorphic disorder: A psychological disorder in which the person is excessively preoccupied by a perceived defect in his or her physical features.

body image: How a person perceives his or her body.

bulimia: An eating disorder in which the person binges on food and later purges the calories by vomiting, using laxatives, or through excessive exercise.

compulsive exerciser: A person who feels compelled to exercise and struggles with guilt and anxiety if he or she does not do so.

depression: A psychiatric disorder presenting symptoms such as persistent feelings of hopelessness, dejection, poor concentration, lack of energy, inability to sleep, and, sometimes, suicidal tendencies.

endorphin: Brain chemical released by pain, danger, exercise or other forms of stress that produce feelings of exhilaration.

muscle dymorphia: A specific type of body dysmorphic disorder where the perceived flaw in the body is lack of muscle development.

obsessive-compulsive disorder: An anxiety disorder in which the person is afflicted by intrusive thoughts that will not go away and that produce anxiety, causing the person to engage in repetitive, ritualistic behaviors, such as hand washing, to reduce the anxiety.

overtraining: Too much physical training without rest, resulting in the body not being able to recover and adapt quickly enough to be prepared for the following training session.

Organizations to Contact

American Council on Exercise (ACE)
4851 Paramount Dr.
San Diego, California 92123
Phone: (858) 279-8227
Fax: (858) 576-6564
Website: www.acefitness.org

The American Council on Exercise is a nonprofit organization with the mission of improving people's lives through safe and effective exercise and physical activity. ACE uses public education, outreach, and research to teach people the right ways to exercise and what products they can safely use for exercise.

American Society for Nutrition
9650 Rockville Pike
Bethesda, Maryland 20814
Phone: (301) 634-7050
Fax: (301) 634-7892
Website: www.nutrition.org

This nonprofit organization is dedicated to utilizing the world's top researchers, clinical nutritionists, and other experts in the industry to advance both knowledge and application of nutrition for people and animals. It focuses on research and application of this research to inform people in the United States and worldwide on the best ways to acquire needed nutrition.

IDEA Health and Fitness Association
10455 Pacific Center Ct.
San Diego, CA 92121
Phone: (858) 535-8979
Fax: (858) 535-8234
Website: www.ideafit.com

Since 1982, the association has provided health and fitness

professionals with research, educational resources, and industry leadership. Its website includes much information about
health and fitness in articles and videos.

National Eating Disorders Association
603 Stewart St., Ste. 803
Seattle, WA 98101
Phone: (206) 382-3587
Fax: (206) 829-8501
Website: www.nationaleatingdisorders.org

The National Eating Disorders Association is a nonprofit
organization dedicated to helping those individuals affected by
eating disorders and their families. The organization campaigns
for prevention, improved access to treatment, and increased
research funding to better understand and treat eating disorders.

National Institutes of Health (NIH)
9000 Rockville Pike
Bethesda, Maryland 20892
Phone: (301) 496-4000
Website: www.nih.gov

The NIH is the U.S. government's agency for health research.
It funds research studies that intend to improve health and
save lives through new discoveries. Its website provides information about overall health studies, including those on exercise and nutrition.

President's Council on Fitness, Sports, and Nutrition
1101 Wootton Pkwy., Ste. 560
Rockville, MD 20852
Phone: (240) 276-9567
Fax: (240) 276-9860
Website: www.fitness.gov

This government council promotes health through fitness,
sports, and nutrition for people of all ages, backgrounds, and
abilities. Its website provides recommendations for fitness and
nutrition to people of all ages. Additionally, it provides information on the best ways to stay fit.

For More Information

Books

Toney Allman. *Hot Topics: Eating Disorders*. Detroit: Lucent, 2010. This book explores the various issues concerning eating disorders, such as diagnosis and treatment.

Peach Friedman. *Diary of an Exercise Addict*. Guilford, CT: GPP Life, 2009. This book is Friedman's account of her battle with both exercise addiction and eating disorders. It follows her journey through various therapies to becoming a healthy person who exercises and eats normally.

Arthur Gillard. *Issues That Concern You: Eating Disorders*. Detroit: Greenhaven, 2010. This book looks into the ways eating disorders and obsessive exercising affect young people and what can be done to treat the disorders.

Ronnie Lankford. *Hot Topics: Body Image*. Detroit: Lucent, 2010. This title explores the many issues involving body image, including how the media and advertisements affect people's body image.

Internet Sources

Julie Deardorff. "Eating with an Anorexic Child," *Seattle Times*, June 27, 2010. http://seattletimes.nwsource.com/html/health/2012221427_anorexia28.html.

Craig Harper. "A Story of Exercise Addiction," CraigHarper.com, October 18, 2006. www.craigharper.com.au/posts/10/exerciseaddiction.htm.

Jeanne Millsap. "Body Image Distortion," *Bolingbrook (IL) Sun*, July 14, 2010. www.suburbanchicagonews.com/bolingbrooksun/lifestyles/2493852,4_5_JO14_IMAGE_S1-100714 .article.

Websites

BodyImageHealth.org (www.bodyimagehealth.org). This website explores body image and offers ways in which people, and especially teenagers, can improve their body image.

Kidshealth.org (http://kidshealth.org/). The "Compulsive Exercise" section of this website discusses what exercise addiction is, how it affects an addict's body and mind, and what parents can do to help kids who compulsively exercise.

Sportsmedicine.about.com (http://sportsmedicine.about .com/). The "Compulsive Exercise in Athletes," section of this website discusses how athletes may be prone to becoming exercise addicts and the various reasons for this. The site also lists the warning signs of an exercise addict.

Index

Picture Credits

About the Author

Leanne Currie-McGhee resides in Norfolk, Virginia, with her two daughters and husband. She has written educational books for more than seven years and continues to love her work.